The Thinking Process

George Lowell Tollefson

PALO FLECHADO PRESS

The Thinking Process
© 2021 George Lowell Tollefson

All Rights reserved.

ISBN: 978-1-952026-04-1

Library of Congress Control Number: 2021918274

Palo Flechado Press, Santa Fe, NM

OTHER PHILOSOPHICAL WORKS BY GEORGE LOWELL TOLLEFSON

The Limits of Reason
The Immaterial Structure of Human Experience
A Healer of Nations
Unbridled Democracy

Extracts from *Unbridled Democracy*

Spirit as Universal Consciousness
The Thinking Arts
Ethical Considerations
Moral Democracy

Table of Contents

Prefatory Note

1. Limitation 1
2. The Limits of Reason 2
3. Perceiver and Perceived 4
4. Thought Is Not Spirit 6
5. The Veil of Reason 8
6. Consciousness 9
7. The Sense of Self 11
8. A Transcendent Approach 14
9. Discrete Thinking 19
10. The Oneness of Experience 25
11. What Is Thought? 27
12. Concept and Image 34
13. Classification 40
14. Dissimilitude 47
15. Logical Entailment 50
16. Cause and Effect 59
17. The Structure of Experience 63
18. Science 69
19. Causal Relations 74
20. Language and Experience 78

21. Stasis and Flux 82
22. The Indicator-Response Relationship 88
23. The Evolution of Reason 89
24. The Character of Thought 92
25. Quality versus Extension 100
26. Representation of Properties 103
27. The Rise of Concepts 105
28. Discernment 108
29. The Role of Consciousness 111
30. The Source of Mental Content 118
31. Feelings and Emotions 126
32. The Representation of Consciousness 127
33. Higher Thought 128
34. Three Brief Topics 131
35. Mental Focus 133
36. Relationship 138
37. Six Topics 141
38. Five Topics 144
39. Arithmetic and Verbal Logic 147
40. Mathematical and Verbal Discourse 149
41. Quantitative and Evaluative Thinking 156
42. Foundational Concepts 160
43. Logic and Will 163
44. Tentative Knowledge 165
45. Plato's Eternal Ideas 167

46. The Platonic Ideal 179
47. Human Experience 181
48. The Birth of Abstraction 195
49. The Structure of a Thought 200
50. Mental Dynamics 206
51. General, Universal, and Ideal 209
52. Logic and the Intuitions 214
53. The Structure of Reason 218
54. Qualities, Properties, and Concepts 226
55. Consciousness and Its Content 229
56. Logical Thinking 232
57. Fluid Classification 235
58. Shared Meaning 240
59. Logical Inference 242
60. Determinate and Indeterminate 246
61. Incompleteness 249
62. Imagination 256
63. Human Awareness 261
Bibliography 265
Index of Names 269

Prefatory Note

Like *The Limits of Reason*, this book is a sequel to *The Immaterial Structure of Human Experience*. Also like the former, it is primarily written from a representational perspective. However, there is a general sprinkling of references to the immaterial perspective throughout the text, as evidenced in the first chapters. That is the viewpoint of the original volume, which introduces the overall system of thought. This volume is concerned strictly with a close examination of how the mind works in forming mental images, concepts, and systems of thought.

The Thinking Process

George Lowell Tollefson

1. Limitation

The most disturbing fact in a human being's life is to know he is hedged about by limitation. He feels the physical barriers. Learning and thought reveal the mental ones. Such a profound sense of limitation cannot be avoided. For it is an imposition made by self-limiting spirit upon itself.

The experience of every human being is dominated by impressions received in the mind. Much of this is what is generally labeled as the evidence of the senses. Spirit, which is consciousness, recedes into the background and becomes an observer and organizer of this experience. It arranges the impressions it experiences by exercising its inherent condition of unity as it looks out upon the narrow world it has imposed upon itself. Or, it may be said, the narrow world which has been imposed upon it. For it has lost contact with anything other than its limited vision.

But what is responsible for this imposition of limitation? It is spirit itself, or universal consciousness, which may be equated with pure consciousness because that is its character. Self-limiting universal consciousness becomes human consciousness. Moreover, it is the differentiated individual awareness of every sentient being. For it is the ground of all being. There is but one consciousness and many facets of its expression.

Thus each individual human being, as a self-limited expression of universal consciousness, yearns for the unlimited

The Thinking Process

and free condition of spirit, which it recognizes as its ground but cannot experience. For it is fettered with the blinders of finitude. So it must unwillingly direct its gaze into limitation and finitude, becoming willing to accept such limitations only by habit. Consequently, its awareness of the infinite, which is its true character, recedes from its notice and becomes fleeting and occasional.

Yet out of this unity of the infinite, this unity of consciousness, which is the one and only unity, comes the human mind's powers of abstraction and organization. In fact, the very character of limitation, within which human experience is bound, could not function as experience for human awareness were it not for the unlimited unity of consciousness. For it is that unity which contributes to the organization of experience by the mind.

2. The Limits of Reason

When a cabinetmaker constructs a chair, she does not exercise her entire skill in doing so. For this reason, the chair does not reflect all the rules of cabinetmaking that are stored in her mind. In the same way, the laws of the physical universe are not the laws of spirit, but are only an expression of some portion of them. Thus the laws of the physical universe are not laws in an absolute sense. There is something beyond them. Nevertheless, the reliable consistency of physical laws suffices for humankind's practical purposes.

Physical laws are an expression of spiritual laws. As one would not interpret storms on the face of the sun as a product of its surface phenomena alone, so one must not look into the heart of the physical universe to find the immutable origin of its laws. It is in spirit alone that the cause of physical relations is found.

Yet, when human existence is spoken of in terms of its physical origin, an evolutionary explanation may be accepted. For this is a reflection of how physical experience is organized in the mind. Since the physical relations of the universe are all that is revealed to human awareness, there is no other way to understand human existence but as a physical creation.

However, such an acceptance indicates that human reason is limited. For reason is a product of natural development. Natural development imposes limitation. It is not unfettered spirit. So not only does human reason appear to be grounded in limitation. There is no compelling argument for assuming that it is a mirror image of all the physical laws of the universe, since only those laws which are required for survival need be expressed in reason. There may be many others.

Consequently, human intelligence is twice removed from spiritual causation. So any attempt by human awareness to look out upon the physical universe and discover the laws of spirit in its design is futile. For this reason, intelligent design can be suggested but not proven. This is because science can only recognize what the human mind is capable of assimilating—what it is able to perceive and conceptualize. Nothing more.

3. Perceiver and Perceived

The human mind cannot perceive without exercising its faculty of image formation. For, as observed by Aristotle, when perception takes place, the organ of thought and the object of thought are both in the mind.[1] They are the image. Thus, if a person were to hold a rock in her hand while closing her eyes, the connection between the mind and its perception would become apparent.

While feeling the shape and hardness of a rock, the person's attention shifts away from the sensations of her hand and concentrates upon the rock alone. But her hand is nevertheless involved. It is understood to be the feeling organ. For she can choose at any time to regain awareness of it as such. She can regain awareness that it is the hand which is feeling the rock. It is, as it were, imprinting itself upon, or shaping itself to, the shape and hardness of the rock.

If her mind is considered instead of her hand, it may be observed that her mind perceives in this way as well. In forming an image of an object, it takes upon itself the object's shape and character. In doing so, it does not focus upon itself. But it is nevertheless involved in its act of perception.

Because the person's mind is involved in the act of perception, it can revert to itself at any time. In other words, it can become self-reflective. When it does so, it experiences itself as consciousness. This focus upon consciousness alone

---

[1] Aristotle, *On the Soul*.
[2] William James, "Does 'Consciousness' Exist?"

is a focus upon consciousness without reference to its content. For the content is the rock or the person's hand. In short, her mind perceives alternately. First it perceives the thing perceived. Then it perceives itself, which is the perceiving entity. But it does not perceive both simultaneously.

Insofar as perception and thought are taking place, consciousness is inseparable from them. For a mind must be conscious to perceive or think. But, in recognizing that it perceives or thinks, the mind shifts its attention from the object or thought to the process of perceiving or thinking which is taking place. In doing this, the mind has shifted its attention to consciousness and its act of focus. Thus self-awareness is expressed.

Now, if a person looks at the mind within the limits of a material perspective, she is led to conclude that the mind takes the shape of its object of perception or thought. Speaking in physical terms, this is how such a process might be understood: To begin, many neurons are activated, creating an aura, which is consciousness. Among these neurons are those specifically registering the object of perception or contemplation. These are both part of the aura and isolated within it.

When the mind is focused on the object neurons, all other neurons of the aura function to intensify them, as if they were an extension of them. Thus only the object is reflected in awareness. But, when the process is considered from a mental perspective, consciousness cannot be ignored. It cannot be reduced to a phenomenon. For it is within the context of consciousness that phenomena are recognized. These opposing viewpoints demonstrate the interchangeability of material and spiritual perspectives.

The Thinking Process

A spiritual perspective, when considered in terms exclusive of its content, lends itself to an integrated unity. Thus the problematic question "what is consciousness?" does not arise. It is simply spirit, the ground of material experience. Conversely, the material perspective is practical. Its particulate character sunders unity, as discrete whole numbers considered individually would sunder the continuity of the natural numbers.

So it can be seen that, though the spiritual view is necessary to a fully integrated, holistic understanding of the ground of experience, the material view makes human action possible. For human action must take place within a discrete and fragmented world. Distinctions are made, choices between them acted upon. To ignore such distinctions would be as impractical as counting the natural numbers to their end.

4. Thought Is Not Spirit

Spirit is a simple unity which is expressed as consciousness. It cannot be accounted for in itself. It is awareness. Therefore, it is aware that it exists. No more concerning it is available to human knowledge. Yet it encompasses material phenomena, which are recognized within it. The phenomena are in a state of flux. For they are continually undergoing change.

Thought is a step removed from consciousness, since it is an articulation of phenomena by consciousness. That is, it arises from the interaction of consciousness with its material content. It is consciousness organizing matter. Now consciousness is a fundamental unity. So the mind could not entertain a thought concerning anything material without employing this unity as an intuition.

This intuition is the intuition of unity. Without it, individual mental impressions could not be combined to compose an image. Nor could images be brought together to support concepts. In other words, without it, each mental impression would remain independent of any other. So there could be no images or concepts.

Nor could the mind have an awareness of multiplicity without the intuition of plurality, which is derived from the individuated character of multiple mental impressions. This is to say that the application of the intuition of unity to some portion of the content of consciousness is the use of mental focus. And it is the exercise of this faculty which leads to a recognition of the finitude of each mental impression. The mind focuses upon each impression and sees it as an independent unity. Accordingly, since the impressions limit one another, their plurality is assumed.

Mental impressions are needed to compose an image. For images are constructed from associations of impressions. Thus, without an individuation of mental impressions, there could be no images. And, without an individuation of images, there could be no concepts. So there could not be any thought. Human experience would be data without meaning.

Plurality implies difference, which the human mind cannot recognize without moving from one mental impression or thought to another. So a recognition of difference is a change of mental content, which results in a recognition of change itself. It is a movement of the mind which is understood in terms of time. For time is a measure of change.

Thus to move in thought from one thing to another is to recognize time. And a distinction between thoughts implies a difference in the mental impressions which compose the thought images. Accordingly, since a thought is limited by change, it is not equivalent to the unlimited unity of spirit. It is material. So it is not spirit.

5. The Veil of Reason

The constituent parts of rational discourse appear to flow in a continuous manner, often without discernible bounds. One concept slips imperceptibly into another. Thus knowledge becomes an indistinguishable unity of relations, all parts partaking of the whole. But beneath this flow the language is inherently discontinuous, each word a microcosm of meaning linked to other words by logical implication. Words can only become knowledge when this logical structure fades from view. They are then beheld in a unity of function.

As a result, they are no longer words. There is a unity of meaning into which the original words were only an introductory passage. An example may be taken from one of the works of John Stuart Mill: his essay "On Liberty." That work is language insofar as it conveys a pattern of discourse. But, insofar as it has meaning, it is knowledge. Could a full understanding have been derived from an appreciation limited to the logic and word definitions of the essay? How can it be understood, if its words are sundered and examined individually?

Reason is often held in high regard as an end in itself. This in spite of the separation of mind from meaning which occurs in a focus upon the structural progress of language alone. Language and its logic are often worshiped for themselves. But it is the purpose of discourse to transcend its mode of expression. The words should act as a catapult, projecting a listener or reader into the inner resources of his awareness.

But the reality is frequently otherwise. The reach of language is ignored. Words embedded in their logical relations are thought to be useful in themselves apart from that which they purport to convey. For human beings in Western Civilization place a veil of reason over thought and discourse and strive to convince themselves that the veil is reality, rather than an approach to it.

6. Consciousness

The human intellect knows what a thing is. It knows what the absence of a thing is. But it does not know what nothing is. What is experienced of this nothing? Nothing. What is known can only be known from experience, though the experience need not be material. Thus consciousness is experienced. Yet it is not material. Neither is it nothing.

The Thinking Process

Consciousness is the greatest miracle. It is more immediate to human experience and therefore experienced with a greater degree of certitude than anything else. Yet it is known only in the sense that it is experienced. For it is inaccessible to any form of material awareness. Consequently, there can be no demonstration of its existence.

Should it be declared then, as a certain philosopher has done, that consciousness is experience and nothing more?[2] It would be better to assert that nothing is more certain in the fact of its existence and that all experience is made possible within it. Remove consciousness. And there is no experience. Remove material experience. And there is yet consciousness.

A human being is acquainted with the indivisibility and unity of her personal state of consciousness. This acquaintance is achieved without her having any recourse to external evidence. It is a part of her experience, indeed a ground for it. Moreover, a conclusion which is drawn from a correlation of personal consciousness with material experience is the conviction that other human beings possess consciousness as well. For other people behave as though conscious of material experience.

This observation may apply not only to human beings, but to all things. The existence of a tree or a rock, for example, supports the possibility of its being established upon a ground resembling personal consciousness. But, in the case of the rock, such a ground would not include a capacity to process experience. The tree shall be left in doubt as to whether it can.

---

[2] William James, "Does 'Consciousness' Exist?"

If there is little empirical evidence to support this grounding of all things upon consciousness, there is none which opposes it. So there can be no objection on the basis of experience to the acceptance of such reasoning. For it has at least as solid a foundation as the conviction that quarks exist.

7. The Sense of Self

The unity of consciousness is the ground of the sense of self. The sense of self is centered in consciousness. Since the sense of self is unreflective, it is not self-consciousness. But, when it does reflect upon that centeredness, it recognizes consciousness as a unity. Exhibiting unity without reference to any other thing, consciousness is found to be indivisible and unbounded—i.e., unextended. This provides the inward sense of an indestructible self. Such would remain the case without exception, were it not for the fact that human beings come to measure their existence in terms of the content of their consciousness.

The content, which is composed of mental impressions, is generally recognized either as impressions of feeling or as qualities of sensory input. Sensory input is understood to lie within the realm of spatial and temporal extension. Whereas feelings, like the emotions they often inform, are subjective.

The mental impressions generate a sense of vulnerability and competition, due to their particulate, and therefore limited, character. For they are mutually limiting fragments of a whole, which are found to be destructible and consequently

The Thinking Process

ephemeral. For this reason, human awareness begins to see itself as destructible and in a position of perpetual warfare vis-à-vis its environing circumstances.

But, upon the mind's redirecting its focus to consciousness, it discovers within itself a character of transcendence and indivisibility. Thus it is enabled to view itself as all-pervading and all-encompassing. This is the condition of universal consciousness. So it is in this light that it is recognized as an indestructible ground of material being which transcends material existence, encompassing all things in spiritual unity.

Since consciousness alone is this undivided unity, it is not in competition. Rather, it is whole without limit. It thus relieves the individual person from his illusion of destructibility. And, in so doing, it suspends mutual enmity. It frees the mind from the annihilating will described by Arthur Schopenhauer,[3] which it discovers to be a foreign element within itself.

The self is conscious. And it is non-relational. The mind is simply aware of its centeredness in consciousness. This awareness is unreflective. Self-consciousness, on the other hand, is relational insofar as it is a remembering self. For memories are linked together by association and are accordingly relational.

Self-consciousness is built upon the associated relations of memory. In the process of integrating remembered acts, gestures, and thoughts, the mind posits a personal identity. Personal identity extends the self in time and space and fixes it among these finite extensions. For it is sameness of rela-

---

[3] Arthur Schopenhauer, *The World as Will and Representation*.

tional being. It recognizes itself as involved in this, and not that, unity of relations.

The sameness of these relations is determined by the memory of material experience. Self-consciousness being the awareness of a relational self, and personal identity being the sameness of that relational self in space and time, personal identity can be understood as consciousness extended in material experience. But there remains the non-relational self. It is consciousness. Nothing further is meant. The state of mind which recognizes its ground in indivisible consciousness and posits nothing further, exhibits a simple awareness of self. But it is not self-conscious.

Again, personal identity is the material extension of the self. It is an identity of consciousness through the extensions of space and time. Personal identity may thus be understood in terms of an individual body with its associated sensations, thoughts, emotions, and feelings. In this way, consciousness becomes an extended self.

Extended consciousness involves past and present events in which the same consciousness is involved. It includes memory but is not to be equated with memory. For memory arises from the content of consciousness. Whereas the self is consciousness itself. Thus self-consciousness and personal identity employ memory. But they are not to be equated with it. For self-consciousness is a recognition of consciousness within the context of its own content.

Consequently, consciousness alone must be held to be the determining factor in self-consciousness and personal identity. For it is the self in its simplest form. The extended role of consciousness is preserved in memory and accessed from memory. But it is consciousness alone that is the self.

The Thinking Process

For it is that to which self-consciousness and personal identity refer. In other words, the self-conscious self is consciousness in its role of extension. So it is the self in self-consciousness and personal identity. Remove all memory of the experience of events in space and time. And the self remains.

8. A Transcendent Approach

The exploration of consciousness can be experiential. Even though it may not be accessible to reason, it is accessible to awareness. In other words, if it cannot be definitively asserted with Plato that there are eternal ideas in the mind,[4] an understanding of the role of consciousness in thought can be understood. For, though consciousness is distinct from thought, it is inextricably bound up in its processes.

Let those aspects of thought which will indicate its origin in consciousness be examined. Thought is finite, while consciousness is not. Thoughts are bound by other thoughts. But consciousness is unbounded, limited only in its content, which includes thought. Nevertheless, a thought can grow increasingly proximate to the unbounded condition of consciousness, though it should fall short of attaining it.

It can be observed that associative thought is conveyed through images, which are composed of individual mental

---

[4] Plato, *The Dialogues of Plato.* See "Meno," "Phaedo," and "The Republic."

impressions. These impressions are grouped into properties. And it is the properties which are associated. Multiple properties make an image. Thus the image of a cat is made up of the properties of color, shape, texture, etc. And some of the same properties may be associated with other properties not peculiar to cats to make up the image of a dog or a horse.

Thus a cat may be closely likened to other cats or more distantly to any number of creatures on the basis of similar properties, while other properties may differ. The cat may also be distinguished from other cats. In making such a precise distinction, one must be specific about the character of a particular cat, noting the properties which it and another cat do not have in common. So comparing these animals involves associative thinking. For the properties they have in common are associated. And the properties they do not have in common are distinguished by the fact that they cannot be associated.

Another example of associative thought is metaphorical thinking, which in poetry exhibits a broad field of play. For an unusual juxtaposition of images sets the mind free to roam over various associations independently of one another. In other words, the mind may move from one association to another without the previous association affecting the latter. This provides an aura of increasing imaginative awareness surrounding the poetic expression.

The play occurs as individual properties within a particular image are brought into various comparisons with properties in other images. By this means, the properties within one image are likened to close and distant resemblances among other images, bringing disparate images into

The Thinking Process

unexpected juxtaposition. An expanded web of resemblances results.

But, putting poetry aside, associative connections need not be confined to specific resemblances. Rather, the relations may develop in a more loose and linear progression by means of family resemblances. These resemblances can be extended indefinitely. As a family, the images will be interconnected through interminably varying properties, so long as there is a matching of properties between any two consecutive images. Thus the imaginative play of the mind can be extended to an unlimited unity of resemblances.

For example, if a circle filled with red and orange dots were to be represented as a mental image, it could be associated with a circle filled with orange and yellow dots, the association being made by means of the orange dots. The circle filled with orange and yellow dots could subsequently be associated with a circle filled with yellow and green dots. This second association would be made by means of the yellow dots. The process would terminate with violet in its use of the spectrum of visible colors.

If these colors should be momentarily entertained to represent a totality of all possible physical properties, then all possible images of experience would be represented by a few double-hued circles of color. Thus, if all of them were employed, they would form a unity of material experience equivalent to the unity of consciousness. This is a crude supposition, but nonetheless useful. For consciousness is indeed a difficult unity to apprehend. And it is in need of some concrete comparison.

Now, considering the full range of properties available in common experience, the associative extension of the human mind may be imagined to begin with cats and to end with a steel mill. Or it may not end at all, insofar as any human life span would suffice to provide scope to cover all possible images. Nevertheless, the total family of resemblances is an implied unity, much as consciousness is a unity.

So, in imagining such a range of comparisons, the mind arrives at a vast expanse of relations covering all known properties and their possible combinations in images. Accordingly, it may come to rest upon the fact that all its work results in an expression of unity. This unity is comparable to the unity of consciousness. In such a way, the mind gains a closely proximate sense of the latter by means of its own operations.

But the imagination may attain to such insight in yet a more direct manner. When in the act of focusing upon consciousness, the mind encounters the unlimited. That is, in confronting the unbounded and indivisible nature of consciousness, the mind recognizes that it cannot formulate an image to represent it.

Accordingly, it is this absence of an image which becomes an occasion for substitution. In other words, though it is not assisted by a concrete image, the mind attains to something which corresponds more closely to a direct representation of unlimited unity than it does by means of the associative process.

But it is a negative representation, a representation of what is not. As a result, were reason to take up this representation in the form of a concept, it could only declare that consciousness is not this and not that—in fact, not anything material. This is opposed to any supposition that the content of consciousness could be a measure of consciousness. For a

The Thinking Process

recognition of the unboundedness and indivisibility of consciousness is derived from the mind's understanding of its inability to form an image of it.

The container is to be utterly distinguished from the contained. For, if the contained is to be identified with the container, the container does not exist. And, if so, the contained is not contained. It is direct experience in the sense William James would have it: namely, that there is no consciousness, but only experience.[5]

Were it the case that experience is so direct and unfettered by a foreign origin, the mind could readily discover its limits. For, in not admitting the possibility that consciousness is something other than its content, nothing more than finite impressions on the mind and the images they form would be encountered.

But there is another problem. The impressions and images which fill the mind cannot apprehend their own unity. For the sense of an individual unity is not to be found in the mental impressions or the associations of them which form composite images in the mind. Rather, each impression and each image is a unity created by means external to itself.

So there must be something other than these which is involved in apprehending them as unities and therefore separate and individual. That something is consciousness and the intuition of unity which arises from its varying focus upon the elements of experience. The initial elements are individual mental impressions. And it is these which are combined into representational images. In other words, the images are unifications of units. For both the mental impres-

---

[5] William James, "Does 'Consciousness' Exist?"

sions and the images they compose are recognized in terms of unity.

9. Discrete Thinking

The free exercise of imagination is in contradistinction to the conceptual character of reason. For concepts do not randomly relate to one another in the manner that images do. Rather, logical rules not only relate them. They organize them as classifications. For in both cases—the formation of concepts and their use—the rules regulating them concern matters of inclusion and exclusion.

A concept includes precisely such-and-such properties by definition, excluding all others. And, once a concept is formed, logical discourse is effected by placing it in a parallel, superior, or subordinate relationship with another. There is, of course, an imaginative role in the process. That is the recognition of associations between the properties of individual concepts. But this role is bound by the inflexible character of the concept's definition, which does not permit any distortion of meaning.

For example, the genus *Canis* contains properties which are found in the species *Canis familiaris*, dogs. That is why in rational discourse it can be predicated of them, as in "all dogs are canids" (though "canid" refers to the higher family classification *Canidae*). For, in spite of the cryptic nature of the associative relationship between these concepts, they

The Thinking Process

cannot be related to one another in the loose, random relations of imaginative association.

Rather, as classifications, they must consistently express their full meanings. It is this peculiar character of concepts—the fact that they exhibit properties which are united in a fixed and invariable manner sustaining a precision of overall meaning—which not only lends itself to, but requires, an employment of the logical constructs of reason.

Thus, the power of recognizing a relationship between two concepts by means of an association of some of their properties is alone insufficient. Nor is it sufficient to recognize a distinction between two concepts by a difference in their properties alone. Concepts must be brought into a relationship with one another whole, though the underlying link between them is between properties.

An example taken from an early stage of human development would be the imaginative grouping by a child of individual cats into one general type. This is image making, which is vaguely referenced to a few general details that have been observed to coincide. But, as the development of the mind progresses, reason limits the play of associative thought in order to bind the process under discrete classifications, such as those now recognized as the species *Felis concolor*, cougars, and the species *Felis pardalis*, ocelots. For these are made distinct in order to be brought together under the genus *Felis*, which is a cat that does not roar.

That classification is then brought under the broader classification, the family *Felidae*, which includes cats that roar, like tigers and African lions. Discourse is thus rendered discrete. This is particularly advantageous when a close inductive analysis mounts up subtle distinctions which demand articulate classification. It is for this reason that the mind prefers rational discourse in practical affairs.

But it is also why poetry, with its metaphorical play, provides a good example of imaginative freedom. A poem cannot be paraphrased. In other words, if it is a good poem, a full understanding of its meaning cannot be converted to rational discourse. For, at each reading or hearing, the poem's juxtaposition of images may suggest different things within a broad context of meaning. Thus there is a necessary fluidity of thought in its expression. This is so, in spite of the fact that there are many meanings the poem does not address.

Discrete thought, being different from this, seeks precision at the expense of range. The mind exercises reason in order to develop a distinct functional relationship between itself and that which it regards. In other words, it classifies in order to objectively arrange. It seeks to set one thing against another in careful delineation and hierarchy of meaning. It does this to facilitate a manipulation of its world.

The faculty of reason avoids emotional distinctions, except for purposes of evaluative analysis. And physical objects possess definite boundaries. They are discrete in character. So it follows that, since reason generally deals with objects and formulates distinctions according to classifications, it may be considered a discrete form of thinking.

It is logical thinking. Discrete concepts are arranged in a classificatory relationship with one another. Thus the terms "ocelot" and "cougar" are gathered into the more inclusive term "cats that do not roar." And cats that do not roar, as well as cats that do roar, are gathered together within the yet broader classification of cats in general.

The Thinking Process

Yet experience is not consistently discrete. It includes subjective feelings and emotions, which are not physically discrete in themselves. Though in the case, say, of touch or taste a feeling may be associated with some part of the body. Rather, they are temporally discrete. They persist for a duration and desist after that. Moreover, physical objects may be viewed in different ways. A leaf and twig are different parts of a tree. But leaf and twig may be considered together as an extension of a branch, just as the entire tree may be expressed under a single concept.

So, since physical experience may be considered conceptually flexible, it is ultimately fluid. This is why the mind initially depends upon imagination. Imagination precedes reason, as images appear in the mind prior to concepts. Accordingly, the mind exercises imagination regularly to expand the power of reason beyond its limiting classifications. In this way, new relations are discovered associatively and subsequently converted to logical form, as images are translated into concepts.

Thus new concepts are formed. These classifications can vary considerably in inclusiveness, depending upon their purpose. But whatever the level of inclusiveness, it remains unchanged for that classification. For example, a pencil is subordinate in inclusiveness to the class of "pencils." But it belongs to the class of "a pencil."

However, imagination performs its operations altogether apart from reason. Loosely linking image to image by association, such operations remain fluid so long as the images are not converted to concepts. Thus the associations can be endlessly ongoing and varied. Such operations are found in the arts, dreams, daydreams, and metaphorical thinking. For this looser associative quality of relations is what gives images their suggestive power, as opposed to the regulated precision of concepts.

But, for practical purposes, reason remains indispensible. When the mind chooses to classify cougars and ocelots together, it observes similarities between them, then abstracts these. Or it can be said that it extracts the dissimilarities. In this way, by matching isolated similarities, the mind simplifies and enlarges the concepts of cougars and ocelots to include them both in one concept. Thus the similarity between them is emphasized. It is determined that cougars and ocelots are cats that do not roar.

But the mind also relaxes and permits a reintroduction of the traits which differentiate cougars from ocelots. Consequently, the enlarged classification is not single, but inclusive. It exhibits two autonomous, partially overlapping Euler's circles enclosed within a greater circle. It is in this way that reason is empowered by imagination to expand the mind's grip upon the phenomenal world. Image associations provided by an imaginative apprehension of experience are enclosed in classifications, or concepts. Then lesser classifications are enclosed partially or wholly within greater.

But the mind need not allow its reasoning faculty to control the entire thought process. Classifications may be avoided altogether. For they are not necessary to mental representation. Thus the imagination need not give up its freedom. It may wander in a sea of focused and unfocused images, as it chooses. This is certainly the case with children and in less intellectually developed societies or communities. Paradoxically, it is also the case with genius. For a great mind is in many ways akin to the mind of a child.

The Thinking Process

Other than for practical expedience, there is nothing inherent within the mind which compels it to convert from a fluid to a discrete apprehension of experience. Expedience is a fomenter of practical results, not an exhibiter of final truths. So reason has no other claim upon the mind than to increase its power of organization.

The imaginative process exhibits free association both outside reason and outside the realm of physical experience, while yet using the materials of physical experience. These materials are the mental impressions and the associations formed from them which are offered in experience as properties and the objects composed of those properties.

Free associative thinking operates in a fluid environment. It penetrates objects, or their mental representation as images, in order to single out and associate their properties with those of other objects. It does this whether it acts in a spirit of respect for physical experience, or whether it exercises an inclination unfettered by experience.

Free associative thinking is the subtlest form of thought, the ground feature in the human mind's processing of experience. Cougars and ocelots are experientially associated in imagination by means of a comparison which exhibits their likenesses and differences. Whereas unicorns are random creations of the mind composed of properties found in horses and narwhals.

Thus association is the operative power in all thinking. It pervades both imagination and reason. It is essential to reasoning. For it is necessary to the formation of concepts, a concept being an association of properties brought under classification. Concepts are the instruments of reason, just as free associations of images are the instruments of imagination. Moreover, it can be seen that it is free associations of images representing properties which are converted by definitions into the rigor of classifications.

10. The Oneness of Experience

Thoughts are the principal content of consciousness. But consciousness is not its content. Rather, it is that within which feelings, emotions, individual sensations, and thoughts are revealed. When this is recognized, consciousness is discovered not to be in any way finite. For it is without boundaries or divisions.

In other words, it is unextended. Consequently, it is unlimited. It is universal. There is but one consciousness, self-limited only in terms of its content. Hence one person's experience differs from that of another, yet is coordinated with it. For they are derived from one source: universal consciousness.

Since limitation only occurs in terms of the content of consciousness, consciousness is immaterial and cannot be explored with any recognizable standard of measure. Imagination can observe that consciousness is like nothing else in human experience. For, though it is unextended, it is the author of extension.

Everything in human experience except consciousness is extended. Feelings and emotions may appear to be exceptions. For they do not combine into associations of mental impressions which constitute the properties of objects. Yet,

The Thinking Process

though they are spatially unextended, they express duration. They are temporally finite. Therefore, they are temporally extended.

Feelings and emotions are temporal. Thoughts are temporal as well. But the objects of thought and physical objects are spatially extended. These undergo change, as do feelings and emotions. So they are also temporally extended. Thus feelings, emotions, thoughts, and physical objects are extended in one sense or another or both. Nor could they be materially apprehended by the mind if they were not.

With the exception of consciousness, the mind recognizes only the finite. Since material phenomena are understood as limited in character—the character of finitude—they may be so defined. Finitude has bounds. Thus it is expressed within the mind as extension. For extension has bounds. So material entities, be they feelings, emotions, thoughts, or objects, are of necessity extended in time, space, or both.

But consciousness is not. It is not discrete in character, as the experience of the material is. Moreover, since everything experienced is experienced in consciousness, the full range of mental impressions is subordinated to consciousness. And, by implication, the entire material realm will be subordinated to universal consciousness. Thus every person's material experience is as fluidly interrelated with that of others as is the ground of universal consciousness they share.

11. What Is Thought?

A thought, whether imaginative or rational, is largely an expression of matter rather than spirit. That is, it is material insofar as its content is composed of mental impressions and insofar as it is understood to be limited in character. This limitation is due to the facts that mental impressions are finite and thoughts exhibit duration.

A thought can be an image which is a representation of a perception. Or it can be an image which is not. Yet the latter is composed of mental impressions as well as the former. In addition to images, there can be a development of concepts which are derived from them. So at every stage individual impressions on the mind are involved. For they make up the content of thoughts, whether the thoughts are representational images, free images, or images supporting concepts.

However, only the contents and processes of thoughts are being referred to, not the cause of them. For, though the contents and the processes are material, the cause of them is immaterial. So, if thought is to be fully understood, the immaterial cause of it cannot be ignored. And that cause is to be found in the intuitions.

The intuition of unity is the cause of a thought inasmuch as it is the faculty which allows for the grouping of mental impressions into unities. It is this which facilitates image formation. Without such a grouping, there would be no gath-

The Thinking Process

ering of mental impressions[6] into individual thoughts. So there would be no recognition of perceptions as physical objects, nor of physical objects as objects of thoughts.

In addition to the intuition of unity, there is an intuition of plurality. It facilitates a recognition of individual mental impressions as finite entities, rendering one impression distinct from another. So, since it is individual mental impressions, each of its own distinct character, which must be brought together into objects of thought, and since distinct individual thoughts must succeed one another, the intuition of plurality contributes to thought formation. Thus it underwrites the materiality of thought by focusing on limitation. For it is involved in the delineation of finite entities, whether those finite entities be individual mental impressions or associations of impressions as objects of thought.

The second intuition always works in conjunction with the first intuition because an entity cannot be recognized as a unit unless it is brought under unity. But, for any unit to be recognized as an individual member of a plurality of units, each unit must be understood as delimited by the others. This is how the two intuitions work together.

Now the formation of a concept does not of necessity lead to a universal concept. For universals are unique in the extremity of their abstraction. Generally, when conceptual abstractions are referred to, what is meant is a classification of any kind: a concept. These come at all levels of inclusiveness from a bird, to several birds, to birds as a class of warm-

---

[6] Mental impressions are referred to in the book, *The Immaterial Structure of Human Experience*, as percepts.

blooded vertebrates, in which latter case the emphasis is not on the entity.

Rather, it is on the concept and its properties. Only this last concept is universal. For it is not about a bird or a number of birds, but birds as a kind, in which there is no possibility of any such bird being left out. So it is the most inclusive classification which forms a universal. The universal in this case is a concept which answers the question: what is a bird?

So the question might be asked, what makes thinking possible? To answer this, experience must be enquired into. And that brings up the origin of the first intuition: the origin being the experience of an unextended unity. This is consciousness. For the experience of consciousness is what makes the recognition of any unity possible.

But what is consciousness? Everyone knows. But no one can say, other than to assert its ubiquity in human experience. When understood without consideration of what material experiences a person is aware of, it is the limitless, indivisible condition of awareness itself, the ground of an individual's experience. Since it is limitless and indivisible, it is infinite, which means that there is but a single consciousness. So individual instances of consciousness are expressions of one universal consciousness.

But every human being will attest to the fact that individual consciousness is found in the midst of otherwise limiting circumstances. In other words, in everyday experience the unity of consciousness is encountered where everything else in experience exhibits the division and separateness of materiality.

The Thinking Process

But let an inverse perspective be taken: everything that is known to human sensibility is contained within consciousness. So consciousness may be said to be more inclusive than the material. For it encompasses all that is known. Consciousness is that within which everything else must find its measure. This consciousness has a formative influence on the intuition of unity. For, when the mind assumes the perspective of consciousness, it is that intuition. Thus the intuition of unity is drawn from the encompassing character of consciousness.

Now, since the content of consciousness can be either enlarged or minimized by the mind's exercise of focus, the intuition of unity may be variously applied. It is this intuition which notes the individuality of one single bird, or gathers several birds into a group, or welds the properties common to all birds into a conceptual unity.

In the first case, the mind's focus encompasses a single instance of a bird of one type or another. Then, in the second case, it apprehends a plurality of birds of the same or various types. But, in the third case, a complete list of properties common to all birds is considered and held in close association under the concept "bird." In this way, a universal is created. It is the classification "bird."

It is in this way that the capacity for thinking in all its levels, let alone the highest level of abstraction, is derived from the experience of consciousness. For it is the unity of consciousness which supplies human awareness with its power of classification. A classification is a concept. A concept is composed of properties, which can be represented by images. And each of these is composed of mental impressions. So mental impressions are the fundamental content of consciousness.

The intuition of unity works together with the intuition of plurality. Considered in their fundamental character, these two intuitions formulate the content of consciousness for human awareness. The intuition of unity exercises mental focus. And the intuition of plurality sets discrete limits to the varied members of the content of consciousness. This recognition of plurality might be considered in terms of a comparison between individual units of focus.

The two intuitions also work together as a third intuition, which is totality. The mind recognizes combinations of mental impressions as unities. These associations of impressions are held in the form of an image, within which they are generally apprehended as an indistinguishable blend of the impressions. But in the role of totality, multiple images become the properties of physical objects and objects of thought in which they retain their distinction from one another. Thus they are apprehended as a totality of properties.

These objects can be complex. For they may be composed of parts. In such a case, they form greater totalities, which are composed of multiple extensions. Finally, there can be a plurality of objects, since they may be considered together as a group. This would be a totality of objects, as in a number of birds making up a flock.

Thoughts are both images and concepts. Concepts alone are classifications. It is the employment of different classifications in sequence which allows a person to unite them into close-linked chains of rational discourse. In other words, it allows her to think consistently at an abstract level, which is to form concepts and use them in logical combinations.

The Thinking Process

Even at the pre-conceptual image-forming level of imagination, every image is either a direct or an indirect abstraction from physical experience.[7] And every concept is a further abstraction from images. This is why it is possible for a human being to form images of a chair and follow them with a concept of the same. The images are abstractions exhibiting specific properties. These properties can be derived from physical objects. Or there can be an imaginative recombination of the properties. In either case, they are representations in the mind.

In forming a concept from a set of images, the process of abstraction is continued. But only certain properties are emphasized when a concept is formed. These are the ones which support the concept's definition. This narrowing of emphasis makes it possible for a person to derive the function of a chair from key properties in its physical appearance. The function becomes what she means by the concept "chair."

The abstraction works as follows. A diversity of chairs is observed. However physically similar or dissimilar, they are associated in the mind according to similarities in their proposed use. One type of chair may be chosen as representative. But, most likely, a combination of mental images of a number of chairs will provide a general representation of the defining properties.

In this case, a person may note that the physical affinity of the chairs is much too variant in character for all the proper-

---

[7] This discussion arises from a representational perspective of human awareness, not from an immaterialist viewpoint, where thoughts and objects share equal status within the operations of the mind and one is not formed from the other.

ties to be represented. For each depends for its relationship to the others upon what appear on first appearance to be a family of resemblances rather than a common similitude. But, under careful observation and deliberation, she discovers that certain physical similarities, which are involved in the use of the chairs, apply to all of them.

So a definition can be asserted. It is that chairs are objects made by human craftsmen for human beings to sit comfortably upon. In this way, the physical properties of bearing a person's weight and supporting her back will be emphasized. This serves a function. Thus the purpose of a chair becomes its principle of classification. Many other physical characteristics are set aside. Only those fundamental to a representation of the properties which support the definition are retained.

The classification "chair," which involves the definition alone, can then be applied to all chairs with their individual peculiarities. So, in stating the concept, it is recognized that what is being referred to is chairs in general, regardless of shape, color, texture, etc. In this way, a functional classification of chairs has been arrived at. It calls up images of supporting properties which are expressed in minimal physical terms: a back, a seat, and four legs.

Accordingly, any exception to this representation would not be considered a chair. Consciousness has been the source of the abstraction. For its powers of focus have formed a unity of several properties held under a definition. But consciousness itself must remain a mystery to human intellectual awareness because it cannot be expressed by material means.

12. Concept and Image

The human mind forms images, which it often raises to conceptual abstraction. For, in contriving thoughts about the world, it makes some of them definitive. These definitive thoughts are concepts. However, it is possible to entertain thoughts other than concepts. These remain images.

It should be noted that concepts are not only abstract, but abstract in a particularly definitive way. For images may also be further abstracted from their character as images, as in a drawing. The drawing, which is a graphic image of the image in the mind, is an abstraction from, and therefore an approximation of, the mental image. Thus it is a further abstraction. This would apply to concepts as well, since they are in a sense approximations. However precise in their delineation, their pertinent properties are limited to the concept's definition.

But unlike a concept, an image is not precise. There are no bounds as to how it expresses its representation. There may be more or less of the subject developed in the mental representation. So the abstractness of concepts is differentiated from that of images. It is so by being precisely delineated.

Most expressions of thought are not images. Thoughts begin with images. But when conveyed to another person, they are often conceptually expressed. Concepts empower communication through their reliable precision. For this reason—its conduciveness to a common understanding—public discourse generally takes this form.

George Lowell Tollefson

A word can represent either a concept or an image. An example of the relationship between a concept and image can be illustrated by the following. A rational number is a concept. For it is definitive. But, since an irrational number lacks definitiveness, and therefore the precision of a concept, it must be considered an image. It is an abstraction. But it is not precise.

Nevertheless, despite the importance of concepts in discourse, it is possible for human beings to treat images as concepts, as in the above case, where irrational numbers are handled as concepts. It is also not exceptional for people to think non-conceptually. Some, like painters, sculptors, and composers of music, may express themselves in non-conceptual forms of communication.

Painters, sculptors, and composers suggest but do not delineate concepts. They communicate through visualization or combinations of sounds. These are images. Though they are conditioned by concepts in the mind of their creator, they are not conceptual. However, they may well be intended to induce conceptual thinking in others.

Thus a painter decides that he would like to paint a bucolic scene. He proceeds to communicate it in terms of visual images. In doing so, he hopes the viewer of the work will not only feel the bucolic mood, but will recognize the importance of it. If so, the viewer will think conceptually about the topic. Or perhaps he will be led to think of the manner in which the topic is represented.

Thoughts are concrete in two ways. First, when considered in terms of their properties, they bear an affinity to what they represent. In other words, there are properties in the object of the thought which are identical to those of a physical

The Thinking Process

object or an object created by the imagination. This is true of both images and concepts. Second, concepts are thoughts with defined limits. They are concrete in being precisely this and not that. This is true only of concepts. For images may easily shift in their representation of properties.

Thoughts are either imaginative or rational. To say that an image is concrete is to assert that it presents its object in a manner that is more or less faithful to what it represents. The image presents properties like those of the object being represented. For an image is a mental representation of an object.

For example, a thought about a dog will exhibit properties which are found in a like combination and order to those encountered in a dog. A thought about a thought of a dog will also exhibit these properties in the same combination and order, but generally with less detail because the properties will be reduced in number and simplified in their qualities. For the thought of the thought need only signify the thought which is being thought about.

That is, an image of an image may be brief. There need only be a few details. And these can be arranged in a suggestion of the original combination and order. This is adequate, so long as a potential recall of the full image is effected. Thus a few details in rough approximation will suffice.

Images must be distinguished from concepts, in spite of the fact that concepts are supported by images. For an image is not discrete in the sense that a concept is. Unlike a concept, it is not defined. In other words, it is not self-contained. It does not set limits to itself. This limitation is achieved by means of a definition. It is what distinguishes a concept from an image.

Now an image is a thought, as both images and concepts are thoughts. It does have limits of a sort, albeit that they are not determinate like those of a concept. For example, to imagine a horse is not to imagine a narwhal. This implies a limit on the image of a horse, and a limit on the image of a narwhal, though these limits are not as precise as those of a concept.

They can be easily and clearly distinguished from one another. But neither of them is precisely delimited. In other words, neither of them is defined. For, though the imagination conveys a unique representation, the image is not governed by the kind of internal restraint which regulates a concept. A definition imposes this restraint. It distinguishes a concept and sets it apart from an image.

To be sure, a horse is not a narwhal. That much distinction may be considered a restriction on the image of a horse, and on the image of the narwhal. For, aside from those of mammals in general, there are not many characteristics in common between them. So it would be difficult to mistake one for the other.

But the representation of a horse by an image can be expanded to encompass the narwhal's horn. Thus it becomes a unicorn, which might yet be considered a type of horse. So an image can grow or be reduced in scope, as when the narwhal is imagined without a horn. In fact, such a transition from one aspect of an image to another is so close that a break in representation is not required. This is because an image is not a closed representation. It is not limited by a definition. Therefore, it is an image and not a concept.

Concepts, on the other hand, are clearly articulated. They have precise limits, as they are defined. So they can be relia-

The Thinking Process

bly employed as terms in rational discourse. The proposition, "some men are self-conscious men," has two terms. They are "men" and "self-conscious men." They are each understood to be self-contained, defined concepts.

These defined concepts do not spill over into other concepts or images. That is why they can be treated as classifications, quantified by "all," "no," "some," or "not all," and linked together (which also indicates their separation) by a copula, such as "are" in the above case. In other words, this is why they can be used to form propositions, which in turn can be employed in syllogisms and other logical entailments.

This is what it means to say that concepts are closed representations. They are precisely articulated abstractions which are detached from any context. So there is no flexibility in their definitions. They cannot be enlarged or diminished the way an image can. Thus the articulation of a mental representation in terms of a definition acts as an internal restraint on the representation and makes it a concept. This is how a set of images is converted into a concept.

The concept generally drops some of the details of the images it is derived from because it need not present them. In adding a definition, the concept need do no more than reference the images which accompany it like a shadow. Thus the concept of a horse is verbal, seeming at first glance to lack the physical concreteness of imagery. But the imagery is nonetheless linked to it and may be recalled to mind.

Consequently, while a comparison of the images of a horse and a narwhal would be required to make the distinction between them plain, definitions require no such comparison. The definition harbors an implication of exclusion, which is that narwhals do not play a part in the identification of horses. This implication of exclusion lies in the selection of properties made by the definition: a horse is these properties, no less and no more.

So now let the classification "horses" be related to the next higher level of classification, which is "mammals." When thought of in terms of this more inclusive classification, horses are defined as mammals. They are brought into the company of narwhals. For both are mammals. But they are not held to be birds. That is to say, "mammals" includes horses, but not birds. Thus not being birds defines horses in a negative manner. It further demonstrates the limiting character of the defined properties of a horse.

Just as a cube of ice is defined by the compartments of an ice tray, which specifically make it a cube of ice as opposed to a communal cake of ice, a horse is a backboned animal confined to being a mammal by not being a backboned animal which is avian in character. (Neither is it a fish, amphibian, or reptile, for that matter.) A horse is an animal which lactates and does not grow feathers, lay hard-shelled eggs, possess pneumatic bones, etc.[8]

So it is just as important that horses are not birds, as it is that they are mammals. Mammals usually grow hair, have solid bones, and do not lay hard-shelled eggs. Birds do not secrete milk.[9] Consequently, the fact that a horse is not a bird must be considered as integral a factor in its being consid-

---

[8] Penguins have solid bones, though they are birds. The spiny anteater and the duckbill platypus are mammals which do lay eggs, but not hard-shelled.

[9] Pigeon milk is something else. It is secreted by the lining of the parent bird's crop.

ered a horse as the fact that it is a mammal. For what it does not do is as definitive to its character as what it does do.

But this elaboration of meaning suggests a problem. For it might be asked, if exclusions should be included in the meaning of a concept, where do they end? The human mind cannot entertain such a vast number of distinctions at once. It must choose to focus upon a relatively small amount of material, which is selected according to context and purpose. These limits may be confined to the definition of the concept. Or they may be enlarged somewhat by context, but not as far as possible. Consequently, negative distinctions are generally left out of consideration.

13. Classification

A concept is a closed representation by virtue of its being a concept. And such a closed representation is a classification. One classification may fit inside another. Thus the classification "horses" fits inside the classification "mammals" and outside the classification "birds." Horses and mammals are associated because they share properties in common. The properties which mammals share with birds are at a higher level of classification, that of vertebrates (*Vertebrata*). So horses are vertebrates, as are birds. But they are not birds.

The contrast between mammals (*Mammalia*) and birds (*Aves*) indicates that there is a distinct boundary beyond which the association between horses and mammals does not go. That boundary is birds.

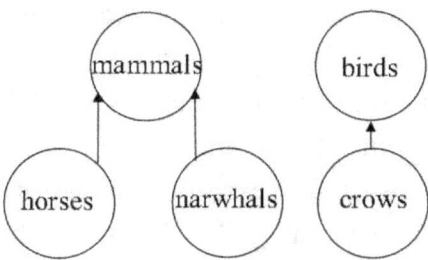

Horses are not birds because birds are not mammals and horses are, along with narwhals. So it is mammals which is the immediate classification above horses and narwhals. Birds occupy a position not immediately related to them, but parallel to mammals. For both birds and mammals are vertebrates. Crows are directly included in the classification birds. So they are excluded from horses and narwhals, just as birds are excluded from mammals.

The concept of a horse is self-enclosed at its own level. That is, it is not included in anything else, insofar as the strict sense of its being a horse is concerned. And it does not go beyond being a mammal at the next level, which classification it does share with narwhals. Now mammals may be included among vertebrates, which classification would then include birds as well. But that higher level of inclusion represents a further tightening of meaning. The point is that the higher classifications firm up boundaries to meaning in lower classifications.

Boundaries to meaning are what definitions are intended to supply. The higher and more inclusive the classification,

The Thinking Process

the broader its definition, the more the meaning at a lower level is restricted. Mammals and birds are vertebrates, which are chordates (Chordata). The classification "chordates" includes vertebrates along with animals having a notochord without vertebrae. So vertebrates are only certain kinds of chordates. And this is part of their enlarged definition.

Thus the concepts "mammal" and "bird" become ever more precise as their meaning tightens through ever more inclusive classifications. All the more is this the case with horses, narwhals, and crows, since they are lower and less inclusive in the scale. And the more precise a concept becomes through such a development of its definition and consequent tightening of its meaning, the more separate it is from other concepts, and therefore the more abstract it becomes.

So this is the way classification works. It provides an ever more acute trimming and sharpening of meaning. That sharpening is most felt at the bottom of the column of classifications. For all the higher classifications provide a greater delineation of the lower. It is in this way that a concept functions as a classification. Such is the classification "horses," when looked down upon through the chimney of related higher classifications.

No classification is isolated in the vertical sense, as from horses to mammals to vertebrates, etc. It is only so in a horizontal sense, as from horses to crows, or from mammals to birds. But of course classifications can be arranged in different ways, so that vertical and horizontal considerations may be reversed. Horses may be classed as fast runners along with roadrunner birds, and so forth. Hence the flexibility of thought and language.

This flexibility means that any particular set of vertical considerations can be ignored, depending on the purpose. For it is only a convention, as in a science, which establishes a classification in a certain way by vertically telescoping its meaning. Thus a science lessens the flexibility of thought and language for use in a specific type of discourse. Such increased inflexibility is needed where a more consistent meaning is required.

In most cases, it is in the general manner that a nonscientist employs a concept because the concept does not carry with it the strictures of a specialized field. Thus, though concepts are classifications, the degree to which they are vertically telescoped into more inclusive classifications, and by this means further restricted in meaning, is rendered arbitrary. Whether they are more or less telescoped depends upon the context in which the concept is to be used.

Nevertheless, however relatively precise or imprecise various concepts may be in use, all concepts are classifications. As such, they are defined with more or less precision, depending upon the degree of emphasis upon their subordinate relationship to other classifications. But, no matter to what extent they may be defined, whether more inclusively and definitively or less so, they are closed and exact thoughts, unlike images.

The role of images in supporting concepts has been mentioned. Though it is understood that they are not concepts themselves, images play a role in definitions because they are the means of representing properties. But definitions belong exclusively to concepts, not images. For they firm up distinctions.

The Thinking Process

These distinctions are made on the basis of properties, which are represented by the images. So, not only are associations the foundation of relations between images. Associations between properties underlie logical relations. However, they do so in a less freewheeling and obvious manner.

An association between concepts is not as obvious as it is with images. But it is nonetheless the case. Associations between properties, which are image relations, substantiate logical connections. For example, to assert that a horse is a mammal—as in the proposition, "all horses are mammals"—is to assert that the properties identified in the definitional imagery of a horse are to be found in the definitional imagery of the classification "mammals."

Nevertheless, logical forms of implication are to be distinguished from free image associations by the fact that they make connections between closed representations, or concepts. These connections are restricted by the definitions involved. Whereas open representations, or free images, are brought together in an uninhibited association of not only properties, but qualities within properties. For there is no definitional interference impeding the manner of association.

Thus closed representations are more limited. Their associations are confined to properties. And these relations refer only to those properties which are either relevant to the definitions or are presumed to be relevant to them.[10] Whereas associations between open representations can involve any of the mental impressions, or qualities, found in the images, regardless of the significance of the property they inform.

---

[10] The manner of such a presumption will be discussed in a later chapter.

The shadow images supporting a definition are the means by which a concept may be made to vary, or become a different concept, when this is needed. For shadow images can be recalled as full images. Because, upon such a recall, all their qualities (mental impressions) are made available, and they are not bound, they are subject to variation. But a concept is limited by its definition. So it can only vary by becoming another concept by means of an alteration amongst its shadow imagery.

Insofar as any image representing a property of a concept is altered, a new image will be developed, representing a different property. Hence an altered definition and a new concept. But, once its supporting imagery is set by a definition, the new concept cannot vary and remain the same concept. For a definition determines its parameters. Its supporting shadow images are the delineation of those parameters.

For example, if a horse is spoken of in the common way, a good deal of imagery is suggested, including "fast animal." The full array of imagery is drawn together in a profuse and undisciplined manner which extends well beyond the scientific concept of a horse as a mammal. For horses may be either fast or slow.

Neither property pertains to their character as a mammal. Accordingly, a weasel, which is a mammal, is characteristically fast. And a sloth is characteristically slow. Most horses are relatively fast, but not all. So speed cannot be used to define them, insofar as they are considered to be mammals.

Thus, since horses can be brought under enlarged classification in terms of their speed, there is more than one employment of the concept of a horse—the one scientific, the others not. So the concept of a horse may or may not be involved in matters of speed. Whether or not it is depends upon the intended context and usage of the concept.

It is in this way that concepts with differing connotations may be employed in varying contexts. The specific connotation arises from the hierarchy of more inclusive classifications with which it is associated, be these stated or merely implied. But its fundamental definition remains the same. A horse is the same animal in any context.

Consequently, to assert that a horse is a mammal is not to indicate its speed. This is due to the fact that its restricted level of definition does not specify speed. Neither does its broadened level of meaning. But, in another context, speed may be a consideration, such as in a discussion of racehorses, where the context determines the meaning.

It is for similar reasons that an association of free images does not function in the same way as a logical entailment between concepts. For it is less precise, less exact in its articulation. Free images form a suggested linkage with one another, not a determined relation. They are in a different context of thinking than rational discourse.

This discussion has pointed to the character of image associations as underlying concept entailment. Through their varying levels of flexibility, images make possible the associative character of all thinking. Thus they are responsible for the varieties of thought. These include imaginative reverie, reasoning, and the enhancement of reasoning through a creation of new concepts.

The flexibility of images, which permits a free association between them, allows for a degree of imaginative expansion which is unlimited. Thus it is a free association which supports poetic expression. A good poem should have moments when it incandesces. That is to say, the imagery of a poem, however subtle or prosaic in places, should lead to an open process of free association in the mind. It is in this way that a poem achieves its power, complexity, and depth. Nonetheless, it should be noted that this free association is limited by the general tenor of the poem.

But the situation is entirely different with concepts. Unless approached at a supporting image level, where properties may be freely altered, they are closed and inflexible. Accordingly, in their function as thoughts, they are classificatory in character. A specific connotation may be achieved by predication. But the fundamental definition of the concept remains the same.

14. Dissimilitude

The manner in which association occurs can be broadened. For there can be a comparison of differences, as opposed to similitude. For example, rather than an alignment of like properties, a contrast of the nonaligned properties of the concepts "crow" and "horse" might be considered, emphasizing their mutual exclusion.

Horses are living creatures like crows. They have four limbs like crows. They both have a brain, a complex nervous system, a backbone, two eyes, lungs, etc. But there are also differences between them in the character of their limbs, brains, nervous systems, backbones, eyes, and lungs. So,

The Thinking Process

when considering them in terms of properties, a horse is like a crow in many ways, yet distinguished within those likenesses. As a mammal, it also differs from the bird in matters of lactation and having fur instead of feathers.

The classification "horse" was initially set forth in Chapter 12 for the principal purpose of distinguishing it from the classification "narwhal." Though crows were also mentioned in Chapter 13. One of the distinctions between horses and narwhals is that horses do not swim under water. And narwhals do.

This is one way in which a horse is conceptually affirmed to be a horse. It is a creature which does not swim under water. Furthermore, the classification "horse" is absorbed within the greater classification "mammal," which includes narwhals but excludes crows. Definitions, and definitions within definitions, are what make these distinctions definitive.

Now, once "horse" is encompassed by the classification "mammal," the precision of its definition is increased. For both the original definition and the more inclusive definition apply. The two definitions are combined into a single, increasingly explicit and limiting distinction. The more limited distinction may be understood as referring to its connotation. For the denotation of the original concept remains unchanged. So the concept "horse" is made more exact by context and implication. For part of the meaning of the term "horse" becomes the fact that it is a mammal. A horse is thus a non-narwhal that is a mammal.

This refinement in thought begins with the definition of a horse. The definition states that a horse is such-and-such and no more. The "no more" is every bit as important as the "such-and-such." But this is not to say that the original concept delineates the broader connotation. It remains a specific classification. But its delineation is clarified when it fits into a more inclusive classification.

Thus the definition of a horse becomes more refined in an increasingly precise limitation of its properties by the company it keeps in the community of mammals. For it and they share certain general characteristics. And these include not exhibiting the properties of a bird. A horse is also not any one of the other mammals, the differences between them being made clearer by close proximity and comparison.

For example, a horse is not a narwhal. Nor is it a donkey. So the horse becomes a very limited creature indeed. And the limitation only increases with higher level classifications, like that of the subphylum *Vertebrata* and the phylum *Chordata*. For it is a vertebrate, like a bird. But it is not a non-vertebrate chordate.

What is important is the distinction between classifications. The higher the classification, the greater the singling out of the number of distinctions for a lower classification. For classifications which encompass one another, and thus exclude other sets of classifications, carve out an increasingly delineated connotation for an original basic classification. The greater the hierarchy of classifications, the more refined in this manner becomes the contextual definition.

Thus a simple definition develops an original concept. But all the meanings of the concept are not to be called up at once. For these are supplied by more inclusive classifications, which tighten distinctions in the original classification by an increasing exclusion of it from other classifications which do not include it. Consequently, the more inclusive the hierarchy of classifications, the greater the delineation of dissimilitude.

15. Logical Entailment

Multiple images form the concept "mammals" by means of an association of the properties which they represent. The properties, in turn, are composed of mental impressions, which become their qualities. So a number of qualities inhabit the properties of mammals. Consequently, an association of qualities within properties, and of those properties within the concept, is established.

It is in this way that the imagery of horses and narwhals stands in relationship to the imagery of mammals. Many of their properties are the properties of mammals. But not all are. For some of the properties of each do not belong to all mammals. Thus only those properties which do apply function as a definitional support for the concept "mammals."

But, upon the formation of a definition for the concept, the imagery representing its properties is displaced to the background of thought. For a logical relationship must be expressed between complete concepts and not at the level of their properties. In the proposition, "horses and narwhals are mammals," the subject of the proposition, "horses and narwhals," is set firmly in its overall meaning. That is to say, its meaning is determined by definition. Thus the concepts within the subject cannot change. For both they and the overall subject are closed thoughts.

The two nouns are united by "and." "And" is a conjunction which joins them together in a single concept: the subject. Thus three concepts, "horses," "and," and "narwhals," are combined as one concept: horses and narwhals. This is the subject of the proposition. The predicate of the proposition is "mammals."

The subject is followed by the concept "are," which is a form of the verb "to be." Functioning as a copula joining subject and predicate, it indicates that the subject and predicate are in a relationship. But it does not reveal the type of relationship. Rather, this is partially illuminated by the unity of the proposition—i.e., by the fact that the subject and predicate are enclosed within a statement.

Being enclosed within a statement means they are united in a thought. But, though the thought is unified, the particular nature of unity between subject and predicate is yet unspecified. For it is only to be determined by means of the proposition's quantifier "all," which is applied to the subject, though it remains unstated.

Thus the precise meaning of the proposition is indicated by a universal quantifier. Furthermore, the fact that all horses and narwhals are mammals demonstrates that they are included within the classification "mammals." Consequently, "all" is a concept whose function is to enclose the subject within the predicate. So the proposition, "*all* horses and narwhals are mammals," asserts universality in its predication of mammals to horses and narwhals.

Below is a syllogism which might have concluded with the above proposition:

The Thinking Process

> *Animals having such-and-such properties* are mammals.
> Horses and narwhals are *animals having such-and-such properties*.
> Therefore, horses and narwhals are mammals.

"Animals having such-and-such properties" appears in both the first (major) and second (minor) premises. It acts as a middle term of the proposition, uniting the predicate of the first premise with the subject of the second. Remove the middle term and the conclusion is formed.

When viewed in this way, it can be seen that the middle term contains properties involved in an association which is being made within the syllogism. But associations are made between images. And in cases like this the images represent properties. They are the properties of the middle term.

It is properties such as these which are emphasized by the definitions which determine concepts. In this instance, the concept is the middle term. So a syllogism does not concern itself with images. It sees the images as properties within concepts. In doing so, it concentrates on creating an identity of concepts.

The syllogistic form of expression which has been considered makes clear the logical structure of its kindred conditional statement. Here the entailment is stated as:

> If horses and narwhals are animals having such-and-such properties, then they are mammals.

The conditional expression states that, if such-and-such an antecedent circumstance occurs, then a specific consequent will follow. This follows the rule known as modus ponens. But the rule may be shown to constitute an underlying associative relationship. Thus, when the entailment is expressed in syllogistic form, the concealed association is made evident as an identity of middle terms.

In the conditional statement, the consequent (the "then" clause) reiterates by implication some aspect of the antecedent (the "if" clause), which reiteration links the antecedent and the consequent together. The hidden substance of the reiteration is shown in italics as follows.

> If horses and narwhals are animals having such-and-such properties, then, *since mammals are animals having such-and-such properties,* they (the horses and narwhals) are mammals.

This reiteration is equivalent to the repetition of the middle term of the syllogism. But in the conditional proposition, the identity of terms which provides the link for entailment is not shown.

Of course, this conditional statement does not assert anything other than the entailment under consideration. It does not determine that certain concepts within it are to be brought into an inclusive relationship with one another, such as the subject of the syllogism, "horses and narwhals," being encompassed within the predicate "mammals." In the conditional statement, it is the "if p, then q" relationship which determines the necessary connection between antecedent and consequent. No other inference is made.

Different circumstances apply to the syllogism. A final inclusion of the subject of the second premise within the

The Thinking Process

predicate of the first is made. This is accomplished by universal quantifiers prefacing (by implication) the subjects of both premises, thus assuring the inclusion of the subject of the second premise within the predicate of the first. This transition is effected by the subject of the first premise and the predicate of the second, which are the matching middle terms. The result of the transition is the conclusion.

In other words, how the transition is effected matters. It is effected by a like distribution of properties between the middle terms of the syllogism. And it is effected by means of the properties of the antecedent in the conditional proposition. These properties are implied in the consequent.

In either case, nothing is asserted about the relationship between horses and narwhals, other than that they are both included within the classification "mammals." For it is by means of (implied) universal quantifiers prefacing the subjects of both premises in the syllogism that the classification mammals is enabled to provide a sufficient encompassment of properties allowing horses and narwhals to be included within it. And, insofar as the relations of properties are not explicitly indicated in the conditional statement, it is by means of a *causal* relationship between antecedent and consequent alone, that the consequent follows from the antecedent, if the antecedent is true.

It is useful to note that a conditional statement sets up a causal relationship, which is usually referred to as logical. For this raises a question concerning the relationship between thought and physical causation. As David Hume has shown that physical causation must remain uncertain and probable, the sense of certainty surrounding it not only arises from repeated observation, as he says,[11] but from an application of the mind's peculiar mode of organization to those events which it seeks to understand (somewhat in the manner of Kant, but less categorically).

In applying the logical relations of antecedent and consequent to a consistently observed sequential appearance of physical phenomena, the mind establishes causation. It is in this manner that the power of a cause to produce an effect arises. That power is the equivalent of the concealed reiteration of properties found in a conditional statement. For it is understood to be transferred in some form, like energy, from cause to effect.

Now there are also differences in properties between horses and narwhals which determine their individuality and uniqueness as concepts. But these differences do not prevent their being classed as mammals. For "mammals" is a broad enough classification to include them both without confounding them. This is due to the fact that the characteristics which distinguish horses from narwhals are those which are not specified as applying universally to the classification "mammals."

Some mammals have horns. And some mammals do not. Some mammals are fast runners. Others are not. So, because these distinguishing properties are not necessary to the classification "mammals," the possession of them does not make its possessor a mammal. Nevertheless, these same unique properties do distinguish horses and narwhals from each other.

---

[11] David Hume, *A Treatise of Human Nature and An Enquiry Concerning Human Understanding*.

The Thinking Process

For horses and narwhals, when set off in comparison to one other, do elicit a more detailed scrutiny of properties than those which are found to be necessary to the classification "mammals." The distinction between them is thus effected by those properties which are not necessary to their being mammals: a horn or speed on land, and of course a good many others.

But, however important properties may appear to be upon such a close scrutiny of individual concepts, they are not uppermost in logical inference. It is the concepts in which they are contained which are pertinent. In certain cases, as in a conditional statement, these properties may not even be stated where they yet have a role to play.

For, as has been said, in a conditional proposition the association which provides the link between antecedent and consequent is not explicitly shown. It may be that the pertinent term is stated only once: in the antecedent clause of the proposition. Nevertheless, the same term is implied in the consequent clause, thus enabling the underlying imaginative process of association.

But consider an even more astringent example: if there is lightning, then there will be thunder. What is the connection between lightning and thunder? Here the pertinent interrelating term is not stated at all. It is whatever causes the sound of thunder to follow a flash of lightning. Rather than make this explicit, the causal relation is expressed without qualification. Nonetheless, an interrelating agency is certainly implied.

Syllogisms are more explicit in their expression of association. But, like conditional propositions, they remain elusive insofar as the act of association is concerned. For in neither case is the association of properties emphasized. Nevertheless, unlike what takes place in a conditional proposition, an identity between concepts is made clear in a syllogism. It is not concealed, as it is in the former case. It can readily be seen, since it is an identity based upon the stated repetition of a concept.

This concept is repeated as the two middle terms, establishing an identity between them. The concepts are related according to their definitions rather than according to an imaginative comparison of properties contained within a set of descriptive images. So only explicitly stated properties are noted.

For example, in the concept stating "animals having such-and-such properties," "such-and-such" properties are noted. Thus other pertinent properties pertaining to animals, such as the fact that they are living beings requiring nutrition, or that they are self-activated and interact independently with their environment, are not stated. They are merely assumed under the word "animal." So it may be seen that properties inform relations between concepts only inasmuch as a reference is made to them. Therefore, though the identity is based upon definitions, the definitions may be limited to a particular purpose.

Now, as already indicated, the fact that an association is being made is not emphasized. For the logical identity is founded upon a matching of term to term. The details of the identity are, as it were, being passed over in a rapid transition of thought. This would be analogous to a string of algebraic deductions employing variables and arriving at a conclusion.

This is what reasoning does. It allows the mind to ignore details, so long as logical rules are rigorously applied. The

The Thinking Process

rules, which require the use of concepts, keep the details intact as the reasoning process proceeds. Thus a syllogism follows a procedure similar to algebra, treating its terms somewhat in the manner of variables which reflect a consistent content.

This systematic process allows the mind to ignore the associative details of an identity. If a particular term moves from the subject in the first premise to the predicate in the second premise, an identity between terms is maintained. That is why the syllogism implies an association. It maintains the integrity of like terms. So the same term appearing twice is identical. In the syllogism, how an association between like terms works is not examined in detail, just as in an algebraic chain of thought what the variables are is not shown until the end of the reasoning process concerning a particular variable.

Insofar as a syllogism is concerned, the entailment registered in the conclusion indicates that an identity of middle terms has been made. It is an identity of concepts. Or, more precisely, it is an identity of their definitions. So the entailment goes no further than to suggest that an underlying association of properties is involved in making that identity.

Such a suggestion assumes, of course, that a logical term does have properties which are defined and which indicate that the term is not inexact in meaning. That is to say, the term is not an image, where the interpretation of the image may vary according to perspective. To be a logical term, it must be a concept.

For example, a color must be a concept to function as a logical term. One may assert that "some roosters are red." Thus the color red is being predicated of some roosters. This is the quality "redness." Now, in order to be employed as a logical term to fulfill the function of a predicate, "redness" must be a concept. This is so in spite of the fact that it is a concept with only one apparent property, the property exhibiting the single quality "redness."

The problem is that this property references only one mental impression: the single quality "redness." And, since a concept is usually based upon several properties, each of which being made up of multiple mental impressions, or qualities, it would seem that the predicate "red" cannot constitute a concept. Yet it must be a concept to be employed as a logical term.

The dilemma is easily resolved. For colors are without exception always encountered in experience in conjunction with an extension: a physical object. And an extension must have multiple qualities, those which constitute its shape, texture, etc. The additional qualities are simply ignored in this case. Thus the resulting predicate "red" is a concept. The proposition might have been better stated as "some roosters are red things."

16. Cause and Effect

It has been recognized that logical entailment is accomplished without an emphasis upon the work of imagination. For there is an apparent neglect of properties in the process of logical reasoning. Only insofar as they contribute to stated definitions is their involvement in a transition of thought

The Thinking Process

noted. But the work of the imagination remains. And an association of properties can be recognized when it has been determined that the thinking process should be fleshed out in its details.

For example, the verbal forms of logic can be seen to resemble arithmetical reasoning. Take the elementary equation 2 + 2 = 4. This may be stated as the conditional proposition "if 2 is added to 2, then the result is 4," which parallels the numerical expression. For the antecedent of the conditional statement must be in some sense equivalent to its consequent.

To explore this equivalence between antecedent and consequent, two verbal statements can be examined. The first is: if the sun rises, then it will be morning. The second is: if the moon is full, then werewolves will appear. Both are conditional statements. Let both be assumed to be true. For, if the statements were not thought to be true (if only within the context of a story), they would not have been made.

The first accords with general experience. But the latter, it may be assumed, does not. Nevertheless, insofar as the two statements are conditional, the fact that the antecedent affirms the consequent in each case is founded upon an assumed identical ground between antecedent and consequent. That identical ground forms the logical connection.

The identical ground is as follows. "If the sun rises, *which it does in the morning*, then it will be morning." "If the moon is full, *which is when werewolves appear*, then werewolves will appear." This associative relationship between the antecedents and consequents is concealed in the original statements. For it is assumed.

Consequently, a logical connection must be made without the identity of terms, as opposed to the clear presentation of those terms in a syllogism. In addition, if the statements can be inductively verified, the connection between their antecedents and consequents will be causal as well as logical. That is, the logical relation may parallel a causal relationship which is independent of the statement.

In accordance with the first statement, morning is simply caused by the presence of the sun. This is consistently verified by human experience. For, when the sun comes up, it is morning. So, on inductive grounds, the sun cannot be posited without assuming the presence of morning. For this reason, there is both a causal and a logical link between the antecedent and the consequent of the statement.

In accordance with the second statement, werewolves are presumed to be generated by the appearance of a full moon. If the conditional statement is true—i.e., if it is consistently verified by experience—the presumption becomes fact. For the appearance of a full moon cannot then be posited without the appearance of werewolves. Both statements, accordingly, would have inductive support.

Of course, a statement may be logically true and empirically false. If the logical truth of the statement is insisted upon, the appearance of a full moon cannot be posited without the appearance of werewolves. But, if an empirical investigation does not corroborate the statement, then the truth of the statement cannot be said to have a basis in physical experience. The statement would therefore have logical validity but not inductive support.

Now in a causal relationship the effect is derived from the cause. Granted this connection cannot be experientially de-

The Thinking Process

termined. It is assumed. For example, if one billiard ball strikes another, the transference of motion cannot be seen. The motion appears to leap instantaneously from one ball to the other. But in theory it is assumed that a continuous and proportional transference of motion occurs. And this is verified by experimental observations confirming Newton's law of opposite and equal reaction.

In addition, the motion proceeds in a vector progression. Putting "english" on a striking ball by spinning it, and by having it strike a stationary ball at an angle, will cause the direction of motion to be altered in the stationary ball. The latter will veer off at an angle to the forward direction of the striking ball. For it must also register the spin and side-glancing impact. This occurs upon contact between the two balls. Thus they are made one: a single medium of expression of the property of motion.

Now, logically, the relationship to physical observation of the two conditional statements above is similar. This is due to the common form of expression between the conditional statements and causation. A conditional statement affirms that its consequent is in its antecedent. Or, in conformance with a causal relation, the consequent is derived from the antecedent. For the truth of the antecedent determines the truth of the consequent. If it is true that the sun rises, it is true that it is morning. If it is true that the moon is full, it is assumed to be true that werewolves will appear.

Thus the truth condition is shared between antecedent and consequent. The affirmation moves across both like the motion of the billiard balls. So in either case, logical or causal, there is an unseen nexus in which antecedent and consequent, or cause and effect, are one. For antecedent and consequent exhibit the same relationship as cause and effect. There is implication in the former, motion in the latter.

Thus a verbal entailment resembles a causal relation. For to state the causal relation as a verbal entailment is to recognize it: *if* a moving ball strikes a stationary ball, *then* the stationary ball will move. In such circumstances, the conditional proposition mirrors the causal relation. This is essential to human understanding. For, until a causal experience is logically expressed, the sense of it is vague and uncertain.

In fact, it is simply not determined. This is because, per David Hume, its initial recognition is no more than a habit.[12] It begins as an unexplained association of images in the mind, which are expected to appear in an accustomed sequence. But then the mind organizes it as a logical entailment. Conversely, a logical entailment is, in a practical sense, a form of causal relation. For it functions like a causal relation: the truth of the antecedent causes the truth of the consequent.

17. The Structure of Experience

The distinction between images and concepts is a distinction in the function of language. But it reflects a relationship between experience and language as well. An image is a representation of physical experience, as is a mental image of a

---

[12] Ibid.

The Thinking Process

horse. Or it is not. It can be a fabrication of imagination, such as a unicorn.

In either case, it exhibits properties whose qualities are mental impressions. Thus the image of a horse originates in the experience of a horse. And the image of a unicorn originates in the experience of both horses and narwhals.[13] For it is narwhals which have supplied the property of a single horn.

The unicorn is an imaginary entity within a more or less imaginary context. Both the entity and the context in which it is embedded have been drawn from the properties of objects in physical experience. But a concept is different. For it is further removed from what it represents, as it is a verbal expression, which is a definition supported by imagery.

When an image is verbally expressed, it functions as a concept. It is definable, and thus can be located in a dictionary. The example of "red" given in Chapter 15 demonstrates this. But, insofar as an image is an image, it is characterized by a capacity to grow or be reduced in its properties in what might be considered an organic manner.

It becomes entangled with other images, which is to say that it overlaps them in an association of properties which takes place between them. It can do this so long as it is not bound by a definition, as would be the case with a concept. For it may grow into something else, as in the case of the image of a horse acquiring the properties of a unicorn, the

---

[13] This discussion focuses on the representational view. Were the immaterial view to be considered, experience would unequivocally be stated to occur entirely in the mind. And an image representing a physical object would simply be an image representing itself.

horn being borrowed from the associated image of a narwhal.

But a concept is different. Unlike an image, it is fixed in its properties, which are clearly determined by a definition separating it entirely from other concepts. The properties are represented by images which cannot be altered, so long as the concept is to remain the same. So one concept cannot borrow properties from another by reason of association with it. Thus there can be no sliding distinctions between concepts. Consequently, a concept is completely self-contained.

Since images are composed of the elements, or qualities, of physical experience, it is not surprising that physical experience itself should be as flexible as its manner of representation. For, as to the representation, there is uncertainty concerning the properties which constitute objects. This uncertainty does not arise from the order of impressions received in the mind. Insofar as these apply to physical experience, they cannot be altered by human will. Rather, it results from a latitude in the mind's powers of organization.

So an image (or set of images) is flexible in terms of its properties. They can be more or less. But it is not unlimited in its flexibility. For its representation can embrace only a portion of experience. Thus its domain is not as broad as that of cumulative experience. For such imagery as would equate to the whole of experience would be too complex to be held in the mind as a thought.

To represent a thought, an image must be extended. That is, it must be an object of thought. For objects are extensions, be they mental or physical. Such an image exhibits multiple properties (or multiple images within the image), be they acknowledged or latent, because that is the nature of an ex-

The Thinking Process

tension. But these properties cannot be unlimited. Consequently, the image must have limits. And the number of its properties will vary with its character and use.

An equally necessary flexibility in understanding the general character of physical experience is due to the fact that its objects can vary in accordance with the manner in which the images representing them are developed. The culminating instrument of such an apprehension is reason, which uses concepts. These vary in terms of the images supporting them. The images represent properties which may be altered under close study, thus reconfiguring a sense of what an object is.

This type of alteration contributes to the development of the structure of experience. As experience increases, concepts describing it become increasingly refined as they are defined in integration with other concepts. An example of this is causal thinking, where energy relations are seen as determining the character of physical experience.

Thus concepts of objects may become individually more inclusive in terms of their properties. Or they may become less so. In other words, changing concepts are rendered differently than what they had originally been. In this way, over time, the intellect alters its understanding of the structure of experience.

As a result, a representation of a physical object may be estranged from an earlier representation of it. For it depends upon how an understanding of the object has evolved. So, insofar as conceptual representations are concerned, they, like the images which support them, are inconsistent.

All images are directly or indirectly derived from experience. But at the most fundamental stage of human awareness, there are no physical or mental objects. There are only mental impressions. And an image is an association of these impressions. It has limits. But they are limits which change. Yet limits which change are limits nevertheless. So an image may be understood to be flexible. But it is not unendingly flexible because there are, in fact, limits to its flexibility.

Until the mind conceptualizes the physical world, its experience is vague. For the experience is a flow of mental impressions formed into the inconstancy of imagery. And this inconstancy supports a conceptual uncertainty, which allows for a reinterpretation of experience. Thus there is an awareness of a flexibility in the understanding of experience. So it may be said that physical experience is not fixed. For its conceptual apprehension may be emended.

All physical experience is represented by images. These images are flexible. Thus experience is perceived to be so insofar as it is represented by images. And, since prior to conceptualization only images are representative of experience, that experience is flexible in the manner of the images. This means that at the imaginative level experience is apprehended as a seamless fabric, which is to say that it would appear to be seamless if the imagination were free to wander indiscriminately over its field of awareness, creating variable, interdependent images.

Where physical reality is represented exclusively by imagination, that representation is carried out by innumerable images phasing indeterminately into one another. In other words, due to the flexibility of their boundaries, the images overlap in their functioning. They do not stand alone with clearly recognized limits.

The Thinking Process

At one moment an image exhibits a thought of such-and-such inclusiveness. At another it exhibits a greater or lesser inclusiveness. So, to a human awareness which is confined to imagination alone, physical reality is fluid. If the mind experiences strictly in terms of images, reality must be indefinite, or fluid.

To experience anything, and, more importantly, to process that experience, the human mind must initially form images. But concepts are also needed. For they break up the fluid character of the imagery and develop independent contours of meaning, thus providing reliable limits to the elements of experience. It is this which creates recognizable and communicable objects for human awareness and thought. In other words, concepts determine that the objects of physical experience and thought are consistent in character.

These concepts do not overlap or blend, though they may change in their integration with one another. So the definitional precision of a concept is its advantage. But the fact that this very definition is subject to change (to being redefined as a new concept) when required by systematic integration, also creates an uncertainty in its turn.

For example, compare Aristotle's physics with the modern concept of inertia. When understood in terms of mass and kinetic and potential energy, the concept of inertia alters the meaning of every physical relationship between objects and, as a consequence, every physical object. Hence the present day scientific definition of physical objects differs greatly from that of the ancient classical world.

For, in accordance with the ongoing development of an intellectual framework needed to better understand physical experience, there is the possibility that, since the properties of concepts have been brought together by the human mind, they may be changed. Properties may be discarded or added, thus altering the concepts they inhabit. This is to say that, in subtle ways, a concept may be restructured by imagination and intellect.

It is not to say that the restructuring is random. Clearly, experience, once established in both the individual and collective mind is its own guarantee of stability. For the relationship between objects therein is as important, or more so, as the individual character of the objects. If one object should undergo change, all other objects would be changed in their relationship to it. Or, if a change in their relationship should occur, there must be a subtle implication of change in the objects.

Thus, in varying measure, there is a possibility of change, however remote or minute, in the relationship of each object to every other, and accordingly of every object itself, as would be the case if one piece of a jigsaw puzzle were to be given a different shape. But, conversely, as a result of strictures imposed by the totality of relationships, the greater the extent and complexity of those relationships, the more each object within them is limited in change. For each acts as a cornerstone of the whole.

18. Science

Modern science, though late in developing its present rigor, is now almost as natural to human experience as

The Thinking Process

breathing. For, given the human intellect's origin in the intuition of unity, it rises as a matter of course to the challenge of a systematic interpretation of physical experience. And upon this comprehensive assimilation of experience rests humankind's present understanding of phenomena.

Science follows practical action with a more comprehensive form of conceptual thought. It is in this manner that human awareness learns first to function at a practical level, finding what works without necessarily understanding it. Then, for the sake of greater convenience, a broader array of relations is assimilated. Understanding is increased as knowledge is internalized under more comprehensive patterns. In this way, a theoretical overlay is added to the practical structure of experience.

So understanding reinterprets the whole through the relations of its parts. It may differ considerably from the practical. But it does not ignore it. It interprets it. This interpretation in turn influences a further structuring of experience, as it makes it possible for experience to be encountered in new ways. For example, the development of the concepts of electrons and protons led to ideas of valence and atomic number, which helped explain chemical reactions and the periodic table.

An awareness of the physical world is progressive, both as a result of increased experience and as a result of the buildup of a theoretical structure which modifies that experience. Understanding increases accordingly. Thus human understanding and experience are found to be inseparable. For they work in tandem, each alternately following the other.

For this reason, there cannot be a final conceptualization of the relations of things. Science is ever-growing, ever reaching toward an elusive comprehensibility. Elusive because no matter how many regularities are established, there will always be discovered higher relations which shift the interrelationship of parts to the whole. Thus the theory of relativity has imposed an alteration on Newtonian mechanics by not only introducing a greater comprehensibility of relations, but also by adding new irregularities.

In this examination of theoretical constructs, it can be seen that the whole comes before the part, shaping and reshaping the latter. In other words, for the searching mind, the theoretical structure determines the character of its objects. Though the original perceptual phenomena do not change, an understanding of their purpose and character does.

Now, when considered in terms of qualities alone, the spatial contiguity of physical objects cannot be understood. For qualities are exhibited within properties. For example, iron's qualities combine to give it its properties of internal structure. It is these properties which determine its figure, and therefore its spatial relation to other objects.

As individual mental impressions, qualities can be examined independently of one another. But they are generally recognized collectively as the qualities of an object. The ordering of these impressions originates from the sequencing of their appearance in the mind. For, as certain impressions are consistently presented to the mind in close proximity to one another, their association determines the properties of an object. Qualities make up the properties, whether the object be considered physical or as represented in a thought. One object is distinguished from another by its properties.

The Thinking Process

Beyond this, without any violation of the original sequencing of qualities, and therefore without any change in the fundamental character of objects, an understanding of them is further modified by the intellect. For an object may be considered separately. Or it can be combined with other objects as a part. It is conceptualization which is responsible for determining the manner of recognition of what an object is. In this way, the active, participating intellect influences the final organization of experience.

Accordingly, the image-producing imagination initially determines a person's capacity to function in her environment. For, it is by means of the initial presentation in her mind of an association of impressions that a provisional recognition of objects is established. But, as a result of a variance in the combination of the original associations, where objects may be brought together as parts of objects, or where parts may be isolated to form independent objects, the resulting objects may come to differ in their final character from what was recognized in early encounters. In addition, hitherto unseen properties may be adduced from observed causal relations. In physical science, these are the energy relations.

Conceptual hardening follows. For, it is by means of a shared conceptualization that collective human intelligence decides upon the final character and order of objects in both the practical and scientific spheres. That character may differ between the two spheres, since people develop their experience by mutual association, sharing habits and conventions exclusive of those of others.

Accordingly, they decide what are to be considered objects, what are to be considered parts, and what are their properties. Should this association of mental impressions alone constitute the properties of an object? Or should several such associations together be considered the object? And what is the meaning of certain repeatedly observed sequences of phenomena?

In either a practical or a scientific case, the thought process is initially imaginative and tentative. But conceptual precision follows imagination. And systematic integration further refines the concepts. In this manner, a series of well-honed definitions irrefutably establishes the parameters of phenomena.

Conceptualization almost always involves a consensus of minds. For concepts belong to the many. But experience is individual, until generalizations of it are shared. In being shared, it is defined for greater convenience of communication. Consequently, to maintain clarity and consistency, concepts are fixed by definition, by integration with other concepts, and by their shared communication.

But there is also a more disparate and subtle linkage of phenomena, where spatially noncontiguous entities are brought into union by the intellect. For example, it is the human mind which decides that an electromagnetic signal, departing New York City with specific information, is to be identified with one carrying the same information in Florence, Italy. Such an identification is sealed by a consistently observed time lapse of 300,000 kilometers per second linking the two observations of the signal.

This is the manner in which the intellect chooses to make an association of seemingly unrelated phenomena. For such broad conceptual and systematic interpretations are critical to humanity's ability to control its environment. So it is nearly

The Thinking Process

inevitable that such reasoning should influence an increasingly wide circle of people.

All the more is it the case that people within a select professional group, such as a scientific community, should approach experience in consistent terms, storing up terminology and a formulation of relations which are observed to occur in repeated patterns of proportional consistency.

From these, supplemented by further observation and thought, new relations are deduced. The process is ongoing. And it is enhanced by the sharing of information. So a conceptual approach of this kind demands that information be communicated with rigorous accuracy and precision. Thus it may not reflect common experience, which is more relaxed and occasional.

Neither are all cultures the same. When isolated from one another, they are unlikely to produce an identical response to experience. This is due to their initial approach, which results in a different development. The development continues along its independent path, until it comes into communication with another culture and has time to harmonize its impressions within the broadened context.

19. Causal Relations

The human mind operates on a fundamental assumption, which is that experience is orderly and predictable. That it is orderly means that consistent relations may be discovered. That they are predictable indicates a causal connection: certain occurrences may be expected to be the outcome of preceding events.

This understanding is the work of the mind. Experience supplies material. And understanding makes it comprehensible and useful. But all the material elements of experience are encountered within a consciousness which, when considered without reference to its content, cannot be articulated by the human intellect. It can be experienced but not known.

Nor is the source of its content evident. The content simply appears in the mind. Moreover, the operations of the intellect are limited by the finitude of the individual elements of the mind's content. Yet these elements proceed from consciousness in a manner which is inaccessible to the intellect and therefore incomprehensible. So, without understanding the source of its material experience, the mind is limited to working in accordance with it.

Through the use of the limiting character of mental focus, it employs an intuition of unity which is based on the experience of the unity of consciousness. In this way attention, as a variable expression of this unity, is applied to specific fields of phenomena, which are recognized as individually unified in diverse ways.

Some of the resulting phenomena involve changes. Changes express events. And some of these events are observed to occur in an integrated sequence. Thus sequences of events may evidence integration in certain situations and not in others. The underlying prototype for such an integration is explicable change, which involves a predictable sequence of motion and rest. Motion is absent from a phenomenon during its state of rest, as rest is absent from it during its state of motion.

The Thinking Process

So, where these states are uniformly repetitive relative to one another, motion and rest become united in an integrated sequence which is recognized as a predictable change, which is a causal relationship. But where is the justification for the relationship, other than its regularity of occurrence?

If, in addition to regularity of sequence, the causal relationship is understood in a uniformly quantitative manner, motion and rest can be made to relate to one another proportionally.[14] In creating a proportional unity, their relationship becomes quantitatively comprehensible. Yet, though the proportions are observed, no demonstrable explanation of them is available, other than that of their consistent appearance.

For events to be understood as occurring in such a regularized manner, a power which unites them must be conceived. It must be conceived so that there may not be a denial of the interrelationships of the sequence. The events, which involve motion and rest, will then be causally united by this power. Hence the concepts of mass and kinetic and potential energy.

So the condition of rest is understood as an energy potential. And the condition of motion is understood as an energy expenditure. In this way, an ongoing energy relationship is assumed. And an ongoing proportionality of potential to kinetic to potential again is enabled. This fits the observed phenomena. But why?

There are two reasons. First, the order of mental impressions changes according to a sequence not determined by

---

[14] The term "proportion" is loosely employed to indicate both ratio and proportion.

human understanding or will. Second, it is under the finite conditions of observation that a sequence of events is rendered comprehensible and understood to involve motion and rest.

These must occur alternately because the limited capacity of the mind exhibits them in this manner. Its focus must move from one to the other. Thus it moves from rest to motion to rest again, or vice versa. In this way, because there is a sequence, a temporal condition is established. For the measure of time is a sequence of events.

Moreover, if such events, being dispersed over time, are to be conceived as causally related, they must be understood as integrated. In this way, the motion and rest are rendered interdependent. But, unless something is assumed to underlie them, such an interrelationship would appear to be founded upon fancy.

So a power is assumed to transcend the causal relations. Thus the concept of energy has been developed. However, this is a concept which is grounded in circumstances which are not of itself. For it is no more than an explanation of them. The causal relationship does, in fact, arise from something which lies well beyond the merely speculative concept of energy. It lies within consciousness. For consciousness determines the mental impressions which appear in the mind.

There is a corroboration between this transcendental presentation of mental impressions and the mind's apprehension of them. For consciousness determines what will appear. And the limitations of mental apprehension determine its sequence of appearance. Each stands in relation to and support of the other. Both are independent of understanding and will.

The Thinking Process

But the intellectual apprehension which follows employs understanding and will. For it is dependent upon the material limitations of thought. However, this thought cannot discern the initial presentation and sequence of events. Consequently, science arrives at a barrier. Because of this barrier, it must develop the concept "energy" as a means of accounting for the proportionally related chains of physical events it encounters.

20. Language and Experience

A complete encapsulation of the meaning of any one thing would embrace the nature of all things. For example, the concept of a chair could be understood as expressing much more than *an object made by a human being for a human being to sit comfortably upon*. This short definition is an expression of the chair's essence, since it states its purpose. But it can be extended in meaning. For a chair exhibits innumerable relations to other objects, such as milking stools, beds, even boulders, oranges, and trees.

Milking stools serve a function closely similar to chairs. But they are not made in the same way. They are dissimilar in that they are three-legged, relatively unstable, and for this reason uncomfortable. Thus their capacity for carrying out the purpose of a chair, which includes stability and comfort, is impaired. They are good for milking, but not for relaxation.

Beds can also serve a seating function but have another designated purpose: sleep or reclining rest. Boulders can serve the seating function as well. But they are not human made. Nor are they comfortable. Nevertheless, they are sometimes employed as seating in hiking or camping situations. So they share a more distant relationship to chairs.

When it comes to oranges, it is found that these do not serve a seating function at all. And they are not manufactured. However, they serve another useful purpose relative to human beings. They are food. Thus they share with the chair a connection: human utility. Expanding the relations further, it can be seen that certain trees are responsible for producing oranges. Others are not. But they may produce wood, syrup, shade, a source of admiration, songbird habitat, or some other human benefit. So they too have a human connection.

Nevertheless, if it should turn out that some trees do not appear to be practically useful, the fact remains that they are plants. As green, photosynthesizing plants, trees help to maintain a supply of oxygen, distribute nutrients and moisture, and purify the air, which benefits humans or those things that do so. These latter benefits are not a result of human effort. But they are essential to many forms of life, including human life.

If this were not the case, it would still be recognized that trees are an integral part of the biosphere, which humans are also a part of, and which involves a nearly indeterminate web of interrelations, many of them involving nonorganic things. The nonorganic things exhibit similar relations among themselves. So the ever-widening web of conceptual relations continues. Looking into the matter, one can see that each

The Thinking Process

thing has a relationship to everything else. Each bleeds over into another until all are related.

Thus it is a family of relationships, where two things may not share properties. But they share relatives. Even the previously mentioned stone provides a backbone for mountains. And mountains send streams down to water valley trees, which are also protected from harsh winds. These fertile valleys support and shelter wildlife, as well as farms and villages.

In considering these relations, a human point of view was taken at the beginning. But, as can be seen, there are many points of view which exhibit the fluid interconnectedness of things and the concepts which represent them. It is a fluidness of definition and meaning. So the bleeding over of one meaning into another involves an interdependence, an overlapping of function and purpose. Thus a definition of any one thing, when extended to its limits of implication, becomes a definition of everything. A complete definition does not omit a single thread of the meaning of a thing. So the meaning of the thing is all-inclusive.

This apparent blurring of outlines does not indicate that there is a lack of order in experience. Experience does suggest order. It must. For order is what constitutes its discernible character. The mind cannot make sense of experience without order. A human being could not function in chaos. So any apprehension of experience demands an accessible order which makes definitions and meanings possible. It requires individual definitions. Otherwise, one thing could not be distinguished from another. But it also requires an interconnectedness of things, allowing for the relating of one thing to another.

Language and experience are interwoven. For language reflects the imaginative and intellectual apprehension of experience. Thus flexibility of interpretation is made possible because things are imaginatively and intellectually understood as interrelated. And, as has been demonstrated, the imaginative and conceptual grasp of them is variable. Consequently, they can be apprehended in various relations, and can have varied functions. For what is understood as associated purposefully in one way may be dissociated and recombined for a different purpose. Accordingly, experience can be put to different uses.

Experience is not fully comprehensible to the limitations of the mind. For it is always subject to an addition, to new discoveries. But that portion of it which is within mental grasp is rendered comprehensible by dissociative, associative, and causal connections which can be understood in different ways. However, any suggestion of flexibility is constrained by the original order of presentation of mental impressions. So variation in understanding experience cannot be entirely random. But neither is it inflexible. For it evolves as it is augmented by further experience.

The process of developing that understanding originates in an imaginative form in early life. But subsequently, with increasing maturity, it becomes conceptual. In other words, prior imaginative experience provides a foundation for intellectual development: the formation of concepts.

And the overall pattern of concepts is further enhanced by a systematic understanding. This culminating step of system building is augmented by concepts like "energy," which are freely created by the imagination for the purpose of cementing relations between the observed phenomena.

The Thinking Process

An understanding of experience grows throughout an individual person's lifespan, where it is progressively enhanced and sustained through culture. It is in this way that it is built up beyond its imaginative origin in a child through an enrichment in the maturing mind of an adult, whence it is passed from person to person.

21. Stasis and Flux

The human intellect works upon the principle of abstraction, or the elimination of unnecessary detail. Concepts are abstractions. As such, they are removed from physical experience. When they are used as terms in logical relations, or when they are employed as numbers in equations, they are manipulated by rules of inference based on the properties which relate them to one another.

In this way, they create maps of experience, the one verbal, the other mathematical. Each map approximates but does not precisely fit physical experience. For, even where quantities appear to reliably describe a causal relationship, they express a generalization which is made at the expense of many of the properties informing the observation. Hence the measure of forces undergoing transition is always an approximation, however close.

So what is experience? It is a state of flux. The mind builds sequences of mental impressions into the integrated objects of experience. For it is in the mind that objects are recognized. And it is an ongoing and incomplete process. It is incomplete because the flow of mental impressions continues.

Adjustments must be made in accordance with the repetition or non-repetition of sequences of impressions. Those adjustments incorporate change because the mental impressions and their sequences of appearance in the mind change. However consistent some of those sequences may be in making an appearance, they are not always consistent. There are changes in them.

So the world is set in motion. For change is universal. Experience is continually undergoing change. Not in every particular at once. But always somewhere. This is the state of flux. If any one segment of experience appears not to be undergoing change, some other part is. And by changing itself, that part alters its relation to the other parts of experience. Thus the other parts are changed in relation to it.

Now the presence of universal flux is a denial of stasis. Experience cannot be encountered in a consistently static form. For it is always in a state of flux. But this presents a problem. Experience is apprehended by images and concepts, both of which are thoughts. Being removed in varying degree from their original context in physical experience, they are abstractions—concepts being more so than images.

Furthermore, when images are transformed into concepts, they become fixed in their properties because concepts are closed in definition and therefore unchanging. What this means is that, as fixed entities, concepts are expressions of stasis. They do not change within themselves, unless broken open by imagination to form entirely new concepts. However, they can be put into motion by rules of inference. For the

The Thinking Process

rules allow concepts to change in their relationship to one another.

These logical transitions in thought can lead to gaps in meaning in the conceptual flow of the thought. Thus new conceptualizations are required to embody the newly uncovered meaning. So, with the help of imagination, new concepts are added to the train of thought, while the old concepts remain intact. Sometimes, however, this process may lead to contradiction and confusion, if the rules of inference and conceptual integrity are not carefully observed.

Irrational numbers present a unique case within mathematics. Because they are incomplete conceptualizations—i.e., the properties of an irrational number are not fully expressed—they are not truly concepts. Rather, they are images which cannot be precisely defined. This is how they are opposed to rational numbers. For, unlike them, they represent the underlying flux, or changeability, of imagery and physical experience.

Representing a condition of indeterminateness, they cannot be entirely lifted out of the general flow of change. It cannot be decided at what point an irrational number is precisely this and not that. For it continues to undergo change within itself as each new digit is added to its unending train of articulation.

Such a condition is a reminder that underlying all thought structures is the indefiniteness of flux, or continuous change. It is particularly noticeable in the case of irrational numbers because they are treated as concepts in mathematics, though they are not. They are images. And only concepts create a condition of stasis. Yet even concepts are supported by the instability of imagery. It is only their definitions which keep the representation of their properties in check.

Now, when a person contemplates the behavior of a speeding bullet, she is confronted with this same opposition between stasis and flux. For any understanding of the phenomenon results in a condition which might be termed conceptual superposition—i.e., a confusion, or overlapping, of states. In other words, in such a case the condition of motion, or change, involves a condition of stasis.

For example, if a bullet is understood to be moving, it cannot be in any particular position. For it is always in the process of moving into or out of a location. Yet, insofar as its reference to other objects is concerned, it cannot be without position altogether. For it cannot be said that the bullet is nowhere. Thus, while contemplating the motion of a bullet, a person knows it is somewhere amidst a general variety of interrelated locations, which are considered the background of its motion. But she cannot assert its precise location among those interrelated locations.

Likewise, when a person is contemplating a bullet as though it were in a state of rest, she cannot simultaneously assert its motion. For the bullet may be lodged in the chamber of a gun. The gun may be lying on a table in a room. And, after an interval of time, the bullet can still be found in the same location. Insofar as the bullet, the gun, and their immediate surroundings are concerned, it would appear that nothing has moved. Thus they are in an apparently static relationship to one another.

However, note that the bullet and gun are referred to as single objects. Nothing has been asserted about their constituent particles and whether or not these are moving relative to

The Thinking Process

one another and to everything else in the room, including the table, which may also be described as composed of moving particles.

Nor has any notice been taken of the motion of the passing cars outside the room in which the gun lies. Were all these considerations made, the bullet must be considered to be in relative motion, even though its position in relation to the gun has not changed. Thus it can be seen that a condition of uncertainty is inherent in human awareness.

The best that can be asserted is that concerning any phenomenon there is a duality of circumstance: a superposition of states. Things appear to be both at rest and in a state of change. For there is always a tension, or opposition, between human abstractions (the state of rest) and human experience, which is flux (the state of motion, or change). Yet this person would not declare that bullets are always in motion. For she would not wish to involve herself in a whirlpool of confusion.

In continuing to speak of change as motion, let another example be suggested. Two chameleons sitting motionless beside one another while changing colors, one different from the other, may be said to be in a state of motion relative to one another. That is to say, their colors are moving. There are many other examples.

For human experience is in continual flux. And the mental map people make of that experience is one of static concepts which, when brought together, describe changing states. But the concepts themselves are states of rest. For a person cannot describe a state of motion without breaking it down into concepts, each of which is in a state of rest. Thus even the word "motion" reduces something dynamic and different in its parts to a single conceptual phenomenon.

So, to assert that a bullet travels from a gun to a target is to say it changes positions from gun to target, each of the many indistinguishable positions being statically conceived. But the static concepts, when brought together, are clearly indicative of a general state of motion. Only the beginning state, in the gun, and the final state, at the target, have the questionable appearance of being states of rest. But this is a relative condition, as has been explained.

So, in such instances as these, it can be seen that conceptual thought transforms motion, which is flux, or change, into stasis. Some particular change, being deliberatively taken under observation, is considered as a state of non-change. For this is a concession to the required stasis of conceptual thought, not of physical experience.

It is a convenient ploy. For how else could the mind engage with experience? Were it not to do this, it would become lost in a maze of ongoing changes at multiple levels in multiple relations. So the human mind puts its concepts into a state of stasis and carefully controls its consideration of the changes which are selectively observed to occur.

The various concepts are given a logical relationship to one another. Then reasoning about them can proceed. This artificial system is set into motion by means of the rules of logical inference. All conceptual constructs work in this way. They define in order to conceptualize. And they conceptualize in order to compartmentalize and control. But a price is paid for this. It arises from the anomalies which continually rise up to challenge every system of thought. For human ex-

The Thinking Process

perience is a state of flux and indeterminacy. It is not a state of stasis and determinacy.

22. The Indicator-Response Relationship

As has been previously noted, the British philosopher David Hume pointed out in the eighteenth century that no cause can be demonstrated to have produced an effect, but only to have regularly preceded it.[15] Nonetheless, it is this regular occurrence of the cause-and-effect relation which provides the mind with its ability to reason inductively. For there is a close parallel between the simple conditional statement "if p then q" and a causal relationship.

In the nineteenth century, the Russian physiologist Ivan Pavlov demonstrated a conditioned response in dogs.[16] The regular ringing of a bell just before they were fed illustrated this response. For, upon hearing the bell, the dogs became conditioned to salivate in anticipation of food, though none was offered in later trials. This became known as the indicator-response relationship.

To provide an example from nature, it is in this way that a young predator, like a coyote, learns that the smell of prey can promise a meal, provided the prey is physically located and apprehended. So it is the indicator-response relationship

---

[15] David Hume, *A Treatise of Human Nature and An Enquiry Concerning Human Understanding*.

[16] Ivan Pavlov, "Scientific Study of the So-called Psychical Processes in the Higher Animals."

which guides the hunt. It also provides a means for the animal to seek and find shelter and perform other life-supporting activities. For the animal learns that certain activities bring about desirable results. Instinct may play a role in the coyote's behavior. But so must this primitive parallel to reason, if there is to be any flexibility in that behavior.

How does this response resemble a conditional statement? The proposition, "if there is the smell of a rabbit, then there will be the possibly of a meal" makes this clear. The antecedent and consequent express the indicator-response relationship. Though for the coyote this connection is imagined and not reasoned.

In a human being the indicator-response relationship has become a basis for reason. Like a coyote, a person recognizes that one thing is likely to follow closely upon another. And such a recognition exercises the indicator-response relationship. But the person takes an additional step. He does not simply imagine. He reasons: if this happens, then that will follow. So an ability to recognize the indicator-response relationship is a person's imaginative response to causal relations. But it also becomes a basis for the logical powers of deduction.

23. The Evolution of Reason

Consider a wolf feeding her young. She eats a kill, carries it home in her stomach, and regurgitates it for her pups to consume. However, the pups must learn to hunt. So, at a later

The Thinking Process

stage in their development, the bitch begins to bring an unconsumed part of the kill to the den and lay it before the pups. As they learn to eat the food in its natural form, they taste and smell it.

These experiences are stored in their memories. So later, when they begin to forage for themselves, the young wolves come upon the scent of game. They remember the association of the smell with food and pursue the smell as prey, killing it. This is nature's version of the conditioned response. And it is necessary for survival.

Now consider Homo sapiens sapiens, or Cro-Magnon man. Does not the same sort of thing occur with this creature? Would not the indicator-response relationship hold in regard to his survival as well? What if, in addition to a simple power of association between cause and effect, he has gained control of his imagination in such a way as to be able to project goals independently of any immediate stimulus like hunger? He can plan for the future. The goal, in this case, is a sufficient supply of food, perhaps leaving him leisure to do other things in the interim between hunts and food gathering.

He can imagine stocking up on useful prey and plant products. And he can visualize it in its hiding or hidden place and go looking for it, recalling memories of its behavior or patterns of growth and strategizing accordingly. These thinking processes, particularly regarding the stocking up of food for future consumption, may involve reasoning. But some of them, as in recalling memories of a prey's behavior and strategizing a hunt accordingly, could result from nothing more than the exercise of an imaginative prototype for reasoning.

For it is possible to strategize a hunt by putting images into sequences and making associations between the sequences. This is a method unquestionably utilized by wolves, which often hunt cooperatively, bringing the sequences of their individual actions into one great associative whole promising a desirable outcome. It would not be reasoning, but something approaching it.

But all that would be needed to change these imaginative scenarios into a reasoning process would be to convert the images into concepts, and their associated sequences into logical relations. Precise definitions characterizing each of the concepts would make logical implication possible.

The resulting transitions of thought would be a more succinct and flexible tool than the associations between imaginative sequences, which must be clumsily arranged in some sort of parallel in the mind, or one after another, without a clear grasp of their independence from direct experience.

A person can act upon conceptual distinctions with the leisure of independent thought. For concepts are of greater subtlety than images precisely because they are more abstract and withdrawn from experience. As a result, the indicator-response relationship becomes cause-and-effect reasoning, which can be entertained in the mind for its own sake: that is, simply as a sequence of thoughts without immediate reference to the experiences from which they emanate.

Such a reasoning faculty is transferable to situations which do not draw upon direct experience. Hence the development of logical implication, as in the conditional statement: if p, then q. The reasoning faculty can thus be

The Thinking Process

employed in a manner which refers to nothing other than further intellectual activity. This is the power which makes a human being a more adaptable creature, capable of exploiting diverse and often unfamiliar circumstances. It is also what makes him a seeker of knowledge for its own sake.

24. The Character of Thought

Thinking is a product of evolution and the intuitions.[17] A recognition of causal relations is clearly derived from indicator-response behavior. But the abstraction made possible by the intuitions has a deeper seat in the mind. Nevertheless, though abstraction reaches a higher development in human beings, it is not found in them alone.

There is the example of a coyote or a wolf recognizing that smell and a meal are linked together in the relation of cause and effect. The animal has a developed awareness which foreshadows the more independent and complex thought process in a human being. But the reason for the greater independence and complexity in humans is that the power of abstraction does not result from the biological organization of the mind. Rather, it depends upon the three intuitions—unity, plurality, and totality—which are put to a more complex use in the human mind. These intuitions pro-

---

[17] This is in accordance with a representational view of the mind. An immaterialist view of the mind would place the whole of thought and material experience under the intuitions, including the mental process which is presumed to arise from evolution.

duce a recognition that related specifics may be grouped into a unity.

Insofar as this results in the development of mental imagery, other "higher" animals share in the process. But they do not appear to participate in the formation of concepts. For the use of definitions demands a complexity of language. However, the limit of language formation in other creatures is difficult to determine.

A concept is characterized by its definition. The definition is expressed in words denoting what in human beings are predominantly visual images. It is possible that any of the five senses could have provided the symbols for these words. In human beings, they are constructed from either aural or visual elements—i.e., the modern Western alphabet or ancient Chinese characters. Behind the words lie the predominantly visual images which are the groundwork of thought.

It is by means of these that the gathering of properties into a unity produces concepts which are more or less generalized in meaning. The concept is determined by a definition that highlights its properties, which are generally a plurality. Sometimes a concept is founded upon what deceptively appears to be a single uncomplicated image. Near the conclusion of Chapter 15, the concept "red" was offered as such a case. But, as a rule, it is a compound image or an independent collection of images which denotes a plurality of properties satisfying a concept's meaning.

For example, consider the concept of a point which is "that which has no part."[18] Such a point is a minimal concept

---

[18] *Euclid's Elements*, Book I, Definition 1.

The Thinking Process

in terms of the number of its properties. Yet its properties are plural. It has no part because it is breadthless. But this means it also has no length. For length is a kind of breadth.

Yet Euclid defines length separately from breadth. For he defines a line as a "breadthless length."[19] Length is made a separate property because it distinguishes a line from a point. So the fundamental definition of a point involves a plurality of at least two properties: no breadth and no length.

But, as the concept of a point is further classified by other, more inclusive concepts, its connotative properties become more readily apparent. The more inclusive concepts are "the extremities of a line are points"[20] and "a *straight line* is a line which lies evenly with the points on itself."[21] Thus a line includes points. And, as determined elsewhere in mathematics, any length of line can enclose an indeterminate (generally referred to as infinite) number of points.[22] Thus a new property is brought to light. It was present in the prior definition. But it was not emphasized.

This previously unilluminated property is the *existence* of the point. The point is breadthless, or not extended, which is why a line can consist of an indeterminate number of them. So, though points are not extended and appear for this reason not to exist, a line is nonetheless composed of them. Thus they do exist. For their existence is being emphasized by their being constituent elements of a line.

Consequently, the original two properties combine with "existence" to make three properties. This point has no part

---

[19] *Euclid's Elements*, Book I, Definition 2.
[20] *Euclid's Elements*, Book I, Definition 3.
[21] *Euclid's Elements*, Book I, Definition 4.
[22] See Richard Dedekind, "Continuity and Irrational Numbers."

because it has no breadth. Moreover, it specifically does not exhibit length, which is what distinguishes it from a line. And finally, it does exist because it is a constituent element of a line. Most concepts have more properties than a point. None have fewer than two properties. But some of those may remain hidden or disregarded, as in the concept "red."

The properties of a concept must be capable of being imaged forth in the mind in either a positive or negative manner,[23] however subtle or apparently absent the images may be at this higher level of abstraction. So a concept has source images, each of which suggests one or more of its properties.

An example of these source images would be those supporting the concept "canine." The properties of a canine would be illustrated by the images of a dog, wolf, jackal, and fox. These stand in the background of the thought and function in support of the concept. For concepts serve as shorthand for a collaboration of images.

In other words, each image in the supporting string of images for the concept "canine" functions as a shadow of the concept—the image being that of a dog, wolf, jackal, or fox. These exhibit the properties of a canine in slightly different ways. So they are further broken down into images which exhibit the specific properties.

Thus the source images from which the concept is drawn accompany one another, though each stands, as it were, in the shadows behind it. They are not parts of the concept. Ra-

---

[23] A "positive manner" exhibits concrete imagery, as in *a plane surface is that which has length and breadth*. A "negative manner" is the use of concrete images to specify what is not, as in *a line is* breadthless *length*.

The Thinking Process

ther, they exhibit properties which belong to the concept. So the concept applies only in part to any one of the disparate images in which its properties are found—i.e., the dog, wolf, jackal, or fox.

Accordingly, in the statement, "all jackals and wolves are canines," the properties of the canine predicate are the same for both the subject members: jackals and wolves. Among these properties are four prominent, single-point teeth, each located at one of the four forward corners of the upper and lower jaws and lying next to the incisors. But this common characteristic differs somewhat in its individual size and structure according to jackal or wolf.

Yet, though these animals differ in this and other ways, they share general properties. So both jackals and wolves are canines. And, the subtle qualities by which they differ, as well as the more general properties which they share, lie within the overall meaning of the concept "canine." But the general properties define the concept "canine." And the differentiating qualities do not. It is in this way that jackal and wolf each form a shadow image which may be called up individually in support of the concept "canine."

Canine properties are abstracted from dogs, wolves, jackals, and foxes in this way. They describe what these animals have in common, but not in an exactness of detail. For the qualities in some of the shared properties may differ somewhat. Yet, in spite of differences in detail, the images of the individual animals all support the concept "canine," without each one entirely expressing its meaning. They act like external buttresses to the meaning of the concept.

Now the images of dogs, wolves, jackals, and foxes are closer to physical experience than the concept "canine." But they can be concepts as well. So they can also be abstractions, or generalizations, in their turn. They are concepts formed from images in the same generalizing manner as the concept "canine." For not all dogs, wolves, jackals, or foxes are alike.

They each have traits in common with others of their kind from which the concept for each animal is derived. But there are also traits which differ. For example, among dogs, German shepherds differ from English bulldogs and Norwegian elkhounds. And arctic wolves differ from timber wolves, red wolves, and coyotes. Which one (or several) of these dogs or wolves is called up in a person's mind when she thinks of the concept "dog" or "wolf" depends upon her experience and predilection.

Moreover, even if she is thinking only of her personal dog, that concept has a history of simplification by means of abstraction. There is a reduction of qualities from the physical dog to the mental image of it, and then a further reduction in qualities to the concept of it. For the image is of necessity an inexact replication of the living animal, inevitably leaving out some of its qualities. And the definition of the concept emphasizes certain properties over others, thus reducing the properties and the qualities involved in them.

This omission concerning the concept involves a sharing of overlapping images which together, not individually, describe its properties. Perhaps the dog is thought of as "my shepherd/elkhound mix." An overlapping of images supporting the concept cancels out the differences not applying to the concept. The dog is neither shepherd nor elkhound, but something else containing some of the properties of each.

The Thinking Process

And, given the probability of variation, it is like no other such mix.

The dog resembles in part both a shepherd and an elkhound. So these supply images representing its general properties, which are difficult to determine. In addition, the particular dog displays individual characteristics of personality which only its mistress has experienced. So perhaps she forms these impressions into the simple concept "my dog." At such a level of specificity the concept becomes vague. For mental images like "mix" or "quirky" do not specify properties so much as imply them.

So, following the conversion of a set of independent images into those supporting a concept (be that concept sharply defined or vague), logical thinking can proceed. Logical thinking can only deal with concepts. Consequently, in doing so and moving from concept to concept, deductive reasoning makes assertions which are determined by means of classifications. For concepts are classifications.

A set of classifications, treated in an orderly and systematic fashion, is central to reasoning. The general character of deductive reasoning may be represented by means of a syllogism. For in a syllogism, classifications clearly appear as a systematic integration of generalizations. Or, to put it another way, a syllogism exhibits classifications of telescoping inclusiveness.

For example, the statement "all dogs are canines" places the subject classification "all dogs" within the inclusive predicate classification "canines." Again, were it to be asserted that "some dogs are large," the predication of an inclusive classification on the subject would still apply. For, insofar as "some dogs" are being spoken of in relation to size, all of these are subsumed under the classification "large."

Neither does the subsumption of a classification functioning as the subject of a statement under an inclusive classification functioning as the predicate change if it is asserted that "some dogs are not large." The negative copula "are not" does not characterize an exception, though it appears to represent an exclusion of the subject from the predicate. For the copula "are" can be substituted for the "are not." And the term "not large" can be substituted for the predicate "large." Thus the subject "some dogs" is included among the "not large."

So, given these examples, it can readily be seen that logical terms nest within one another. For logical thinking does not operate upon a diffuse and disordered arrangement, as does imaginative thinking. Rather, the original mental impressions of such a thought process are gleaned from qualities expressed in physical experience, and are gathered into representational images which are similar to but less refulgent than an object of perception.[24] These images, in turn, form the supporting properties of conceptual classifications. All this takes place prior to reasoning. For it is these classifications which are employed in reasoning.

Now the inductive process initially concerns physical events, as opposed to objects not undergoing change. So, should such an event be observed in terms of a sequence of images, and subsequently be represented conceptually (and

---

[24] As previously mentioned, this is being considered under a representational view, which, for convenience sake, treats physical objects as things-in-themselves.

The Thinking Process

therefore statically), it would be in terms of a relationship representing a change in the location of a physical object or in terms of a change within one. Thus, as it moves from imagery to the concept of a relation, induction occurs prior to deductive reasoning. For it translates physical events into conceptual thought.

25. Quality versus Extension

Physical objects are physical extensions. Mental objects are mental extensions. Extensions involve a plurality of mental impressions. These associated impressions take the form of representations, or images, in the mind. For the mind focuses on multiple mental impressions as qualities of objects. But individual mental impressions can also occur independently. When they do, they represent feelings.

An image is a mental object. When the mind focuses upon a physical object, it does so by means of a mental object. The mental object *is* the physical object. Or, if the physical object is understood to be complex, the mental object approximates it. And it is a series of mental objects which *are* the physical object. But the experience of an individual quality is the experience of a feeling. It is not an object. For there must be an image to represent an object.

So the multiple qualities of objects, though each can be briefly experienced by the mind, are represented in association with one another to form mental extensions as images. It is these images which, when repeated, are retained in thought. Otherwise, though fleetingly present to human awareness, individual mental impressions vanish from thought and cannot enter into any of its processes.

For example, sweetness and roundness pertain to a peach. But, unlike the composite of mental impressions which delineate the property "roundness," "sweetness" is expressed by a single impression. It is a constituent of taste. And to taste something is to encounter the presence of that taste in a body.

In other words, the sweetness of a peach expresses something about the extended fruit, just as figure does. If the peach were not extended, it could not reasonably be conceived to provide the sweetness. For this is the consistent testimony of experience. Qualities appear within the extensions of objects. They do not appear in representational experience independently of an object.

A physical object occupies a location. It is therefore extended. It occupies space. Or, more accurately, it participates with other objects in constructing space. For two or more extensions are not coterminous. So a physical object has a specific location vis-à-vis any other physical object. Thus, for the object's location to be usurped by another object, it must be displaced. The requirement of its being displaced is its extension, which is spatially expressed by its figure. And experience teaches the universal character of extension. For, though objects are encountered as images in the mind, there is a mental supposition of the extension of the object.

Figure is different from quality. For it is not experienced as a single mental impression. It involves a plurality of impressions. The roundness of a peach exhibits multiple points of address, which various impressions together constitute the

The Thinking Process

figure. So to say a physical object has a shape is to assert that it does so by means of its being an extension. In other words, for something to be an extension is to say it exhibits figure. So extension implies shape. And shape implies extension.

Unlike a quality such as sweetness, the figure, or roundness, of a peach stands independently in the mind as a thought extension. This is demonstrated by the fact that, in spite of its character as an idealized abstraction, a circle, a triangle, a square, or any other geometrical figure must be imagined as an extension. Albeit that it is an extension without qualities other than those of figure.

Sweetness does not appear to the mind in this manner. For, when referenced alone as a single mental impression, it cannot be held in the mind as an image. This is because it is not imagined as involved in an extension. In other words, while it is true that a person can in some sense recall one sweet taste as like or unlike another, it is but a fleeting impression which cannot be held in thought. Rather, to be so, it must be imagined as inhabiting an extension. That is to say, it must be accompanied in thought by a multiple of mental impressions. For these are what make an extension. And a mental image is an extension.

So the difference between figure and an isolated quality is due to the fact that figure is a function of extension. In other words, figure *is* extension, or a series of extensions as parts. Whereas a single quality is insufficient to constitute an extension. In other words, if sweetness is to be represented to the mind, something extended having the quality of sweetness must be thought of. For sweetness alone has no necessary connection with extension.

Conversely, figure cannot be spoken of without suggesting extension. Nor can extension be mentioned without suggesting figure. Whereas, in referring to sweetness alone, a person omits any suggestion of extension. But, if she wishes to embody sweetness in a mental image, she must reference the experience of an object, even if the object be nothing more than her tongue.

A single quality is more mentally distinct than is a figure. For it is a mental impression. Whereas the awareness of figure, as in a recognition of the roundness of a peach, arises from an association of multiple impressions in which no one impression achieves a dominance of mental focus. The association becomes more prominent in the mind than the individual qualities.

26. Representation of Properties

When it is a direct expression of properties, a set of images is roughly equivalent to the object it represents. For the combined properties are those of the object. However, the properties exhibit less than a full representation because the object may present itself to the mind in multiple ways. That is, different images may represent alternate facets of the properties. Thus any set of them is reduced to an approximation, exhibiting certain aspects of the properties and leaving out others.

Due to its increased level of abstraction, a concept of an object will be even further removed from it than the repre-

The Thinking Process

sentational imagery. The concept's limiting definition involves a reduction of properties so that precise associations can be facilitated. For the smaller the number of properties under consideration, the more accessible the thought is to reason. In addition, when only a few properties are being associated between concepts, some of the definitional properties will be set aside as well. This occurs when a horse is associated with mammals. Only its mammalian properties are considered.

Images and concepts which are created by the imagination are different than images and concepts which are representational. For they are composed of properties taken from various unrelated objects and combined in a new way. Hence, as a result of their arbitrary construction, though the new images or concepts will exhibit properties drawn from those encountered in material experience, they will not represent the original objects.

Logical relations between concepts are made whether an association between properties involved in the relations is discernible or assumed. For in syllogistic reasoning, establishing an association is the role of propositions, which exhibit relationships between subject and predicate. Other types of statements follow a similar pattern. For this reason, one concept may be predicated of another without an apparent association of properties, as exemplified in "all royalty is housed in cheap apartments," and "if they are royals, then they are housed in cheap apartments."

These statements are not empirically true. For the majority of royals have been well accommodated. So, clearly, observation has been set aside in making the assertion. Yet, so long as logical consistency is maintained, the assumption can be carried forward in a reasoning process. Thus the assertion can be logically true without being empirically so.

But a statement such as "horses are mammals" is founded upon a recognition of kindred properties in both subject and predicate. For these are what make the horses mammals. They are verified by observation. Thus, since the association between subject and predicate is affirmed on the basis of horses having the properties of mammals, the statement is considered empirically true.

27. The Rise of Concepts

A concept for dogs is likely to have developed on the basis of a number of them having been observed at various times in different places. The concept was formed so that the observation could be made available to a reasoning process. The concept is a classification. Prior to its development, an image would have been formed upon the first encounter with a dog.

After multiple such encounters with the same or different dogs, the formation of closely related images would have occurred. The images could then have merged into an overlapping family of images. Following this, they would have been narrowed toward the fixing of a definition in a closed thought: a concept.

The individual images are considered to be open thoughts due to their imprecision and consequent flexibility. As opposed to this, a concept is considered closed because it is

The Thinking Process

more precise and lacks the imprecision and flexibility of an image. Hence the denomination used for a concept: a closed thought.[25]

Once having been formed, the concept of a dog is stored in memory, as was previously the case with the various images of dogs. When a dog is subsequently encountered, it is recognized by means of the set of images previously stored in memory. But these now reference a concept. So it is the concept which is recalled from memory. Accordingly, a dog is identified as an entity which has a precise definition.

Both the images and the concept are thought extensions, which are associations of multiple mental impressions. They have this in common. But the concept differs from the image in that it is made more precise than the image by means of a definition which highlights its salient properties.

However, new encounters are likely to be made. So an additional physical or behavioral feature may be observed which had not been previously noted. If it is confirmed in terms of a number of observations of different dogs, and if it is found to be characteristic of dogs in general, it must be reckoned with conceptually.

Because the feature is new to the observer and is being encountered post definition, it is discovered without the aid

---

[25] Note that a set of images is sometimes referred to as a single image: a single open thought. This practice also includes the set of images supporting a concept, in which the concept is referred to as a single closed thought. The practice is justified by the fact that the mind may use a single simplified image to represent a set of images which is either independent of or in support of a concept. Each image of a set may also be, in turn, a simplified representation of another set of images. For an image can have properties which are images. And properties can have properties, particularly when qualities are taken under consideration as properties.

of the original images or concepts lodged in memory. That is to say, it is observed on the basis of immediate mental impressions. Each such encounter will contribute a new image to the mind of the observer. Thus repeated observations of a phenomenon will form related images.

The association of properties already held in memory as defining the original concept will constitute past experience. It will be called forth and brought into a relationship with the new feature which is destined to amend it. Say the following is a new property: if treated well, dogs will exhibit loyal behavior. The concept "dogs" will thus be broadened to include the additional property.

This fusing of a fresh observation with a prior concept is the process of induction. Forming an induction is not a part of any reasoning process. For reasoning is deduction. So induction occurs prior to deductive reasoning. It is in this way that the concept "dogs" would be amended to include loyalty, the inductive observation being joined with other already acknowledged properties in modifying an existing concept.

Any addition of properties to an existing concept indicates image augmentation. For definitions depend upon images. Comparing concepts, as in comparing dogs to wolves and foxes, points up the fact that dogs readily form bonds with humans, while wolves and foxes do not. So further observation, or induction, has broadened a definition, yet made it more precise.

All concepts, even the most abstract, rely upon observation for their content. For a concept which is imaginatively developed can only be constructed from mental impressions derived from experience. A mathematical concept, like a perfect circle, may be imaginatively invented through a process

The Thinking Process

of stripping away most of a physical circle's material properties. But a perfect circle will not be encountered in physical experience. Yet it can be visualized because phenomena such as the sun, moon, and wheels have been observed. Imagination has simply removed irregularities in curvature to suggest one that is uniform.

28. Discernment

A recognition of specifics is necessary to the successful functioning of a sentient organism. For information is internalized as associated bundles of mental impressions which are identified as physical objects or their properties. In addition, there is a sense of events, or successive changes in the relations or condition of objects. So the ability to identify objects, groups of objects, and events which might indicate behavioral characteristics in other organisms, is a necessary faculty. For this reason, it is present in varying degree in all sentient life forms.[26]

Thus a dog not only recognizes its owner. It identifies other people as not being its owner. For, aside from the ruder evidences of smell, sight, and sound, it knows that its owner is the one who feeds it. This latter type of discernment is based upon expected behavior, which entails both a recognition of specifics and a more complex and meaningful

---

[26] Even a carnivorous plant must recognize the presence of an insect. But whether or not this implies an active intelligence, however rudimentary, is open to debate.

awareness of sequences of events. In some cases much of this faculty may take the form of instinct in lower forms. But there is always some individual discernment.

Discernment is an acute faculty in human beings. Nevertheless, conceptualization and a logical manipulation of concepts, which are associated with the exercise of reason, are variants of a presumably lesser faculty in other higher life forms. Insofar as is known, dogs work exclusively with images. Whereas people do similar things more efficiently with concepts.

Consciousness and the fundamental operations of thought, like association and the bare rudiments of induction, are present in other animals, but in simpler form. An ant can recognize food. In its search for it, it can explore, discover resources, and communicate various prospects and dangers to its nest mates.

This is not entirely instinct. Even where it is, the instinct might be referred to as ossified discernment. It is inheritable habit. In other words, certain patterns of discernment become innate and are regularly repeated from generation to generation. But not all of an ant's behavior is determined in this manner. Were that so, it could not survive. For the exigencies of life are remarkably variable and unpredictable.

Thought is more developed in the higher life forms. But at all levels of sentient life there is the peculiar biology of the organism, influencing the complexity of its awareness. However, biology is at issue only in determining the scope, not the underlying possibility, of intelligent behavior. Whatever an organism's level of sophistication in assimilating the data of experience, however circumscribed this may be in some cases, to be sentient at all, it must be conscious. It must make

The Thinking Process

choices. For it must have at least some flexibility in its responses to its environment.

An ant possesses far too complex a behavioral dynamic for the creature to be dismissed as an automaton. Upon close inspection, it becomes readily apparent that its behavior exhibits a good deal more than an array of instinctive responses. There will always be some mystery in what it does. For its behavior cannot be subjectively understood. But it can be said to exhibit some form of mental life, to express a degree of intelligence, albeit that its intelligence is quite rudimentary and unaccompanied by reason.

So it may be asked, why is there a prejudice against other sentient life forms, particularly the simpler ones? Why have they been reduced to automata? It is because a human being exists as though sealed in an impermeable body of experience and consequently knows only it. She recognizes the complex dynamic of awareness in herself and attributes a soul to herself in explanation of it. She also attributes a soul to those other creatures most resembling herself: other people. But she generally neglects to do the same for many other organisms, particularly those which appear to be simplest in organization.

If these considerations are not sufficient, a person might, by looking inward, recognize a rich complexity of awareness, much of which is neither attributable to, nor explainable by, reason. Knowing this, how can she with any assurance deny the possibility of such a faculty in another creature capable of responding to stimuli?

29. The Role of Consciousness

The recognition of individual mental impressions and the bringing of them into association with one another, which characterizes both image formation and the abstraction of images into concepts, clearly exhibits an extra-biological character. For the mental powers facilitating such a recognition and organization are rendered possible by consciousness.

Consciousness experiences itself as indivisible, unextended, and unlimited. Thus it is immaterial. For divisibility, extension, and limitation are material characteristics. Consciousness is a unity. And that unity, when experienced, is the origin of the intuition of unity in human awareness. There must be a similar mode of awareness in any other sentient life form. For this intuition is the faculty which facilitates the recognition of mental impressions and the unifying of them into images representing objects.

Consciousness apprehends itself as immaterial. As it is without division or bounds, it is without measurable parts. It is for this reason that it is recognized as infinite, or *not* finite. That is what the word *in*finite means. It means without extent or limits, and therefore without parts. It does not mean extended indefinitely or indefinitely divisible. For this would imply immeasurable parts, which would not be finite.

Infinitude and finitude are mutually exclusive conditions. So anything finite must be composed of finite parts. Whether those parts are conceived to be indeterminately large in number or indeterminately small in size, does not alter either

The Thinking Process

their collective or their individual finitude. In either case, they cannot be thought to be compounded into an infinity.

So, insofar as consciousness is concerned, it may be said to recognize itself as something other than an entity limited by other entities. Mind, on the other hand, exhibits states of consciousness, each being one among many mutually exclusive modes expressing limited duration. A state of mind is not consciousness as such. For, unlike consciousness, it is finite in that it might be a limited state of pleasure or pain, of fear or anger, peace or joy, or a complex mix of such experiences. In other words, a state of mind is finite because it is experienced as exhibiting duration.

Consciousness exhibits none of these forms of limitation. When experienced in terms of itself, and not its content, it is utterly estranged from any kind of measure. So, though it may be spoken of as terminating in physical death, this is merely an expression of speech. For it is not consciousness which is understood to terminate.

Rather, it is physical life which is spoken of in this manner. Physical life is understood to terminate because it has duration. And, having duration, it is finite. To be finite is to be limited physically and temporally. For this reason, only a finite entity can express a limited character. Consciousness is not a finite entity.

Consciousness, when considered in combination with its finite content, produces a hybrid condition which exhibits features that are both finite and infinite. The human mind is such a hybrid. It is finite in its content of mental impressions and infinite in consciousness. For a like reason, thought extensions, as well as physical extensions (which are experienced as thought extensions), are also hybrids. For their content is finite. But the unity of their form is determined by a reference to the unity of consciousness.

A mental image's power of combining properties, and a concept's power of the classification of the same, are derived from consciousness by means of the intuition of unity. Whereas the mental impressions composing the properties are the content of consciousness. In other words, an image and a concept are composed of properties, which are, in turn, composed of mental impressions. But the image and concept are the means by which these properties are held in association.

This is accomplished in a deliberate manner. In other words, from a representational point of view,[27] image and concept formation may be understood to result from acts of the will. These are not only simple, but complex, acts in which a person exercises his full imaginative and reasoning processes, building thought upon thought.

So it can be said that images and concepts are formed by an immaterial process which unifies their properties. But in asserting this, it should be noted that it is mental impressions which establish the content of consciousness. They alone are the substance of material experience. In the language of common discourse, they would be called sensations.

Since mental impressions originate in the mind independently of the will, they cannot be removed from

---

[27] The representational point of view is taken from the limited perspective of an individual person's awareness. The more encompassing immaterial perspective enunciated in *The Immaterial Structure of Human Experience* and expressed in a few instances here is generally set aside in the overall development of this work, while not being denied at any point.

The Thinking Process

experience. But they may be variously combined into imagery. Having become images, they can be further refined into a concept. So mental impressions may be brought together within an image or concept to form a finite mental extension which is an association of impressions: a thought.

Physical objects are mental extensions as well. They are experienced as mental impressions and the images they collectively compose. From an immaterial perspective, the order in which they appear in the mind would be fixed. For, when understood transcendentally, all the content of consciousness is received in a determined order within consciousness.

Thus all physical objects would be encountered only as predetermined mental images. And an act of the will must then be understood as something which occurs in consciousness prior to material experience. For the immaterial perspective is free of the constraints of time. The whole of life thus becomes an aftereffect of an instantaneous movement of the will.

But, from a individual person's representational point of view, the order of mental impressions appears to be determined by his will as it is exercised within the material context. For the physical realm is then understood to be independent of the perceiving mind. Thus it is a person's presently active will which is felt to establish the order in which impressions are perceived, as when he considers an object from top to bottom as opposed to experiencing it from bottom to top.

In either an immaterial or a representational case, mental images are associations of mental impressions gathered into a unity. And, insofar as they are recognized within a representational context, they can be understood as being founded upon the intuition of unity. A classification, or concept—which is derived from imagery—is also a finite unity. So it must be asked in what manner it is that such unities become finite within a representational context.

This could not occur, unless the intuition of unity were accompanied by another intuition conferring finitude. That intuition is plurality. It is a product of material experience. For, in distinguishing individual mental impressions, like red and blue, the mind recognizes their mutual limits—i.e., that one is not the other.

They can be identified independently of one another and are found to limit one another in experience. These characteristics of independence and mutual limitation result from the fact that the mind focuses upon one, then the other. That focus is an exercise of the intuition of unity. But a recognition of the distinction it creates is an exercise of the intuition of plurality.

So the intuition of plurality is grounded in a recognition of the unique and limited character of each mental impression. It subsequently extends its influence to multiple mental impressions apprehended in association with one another. It does this by working in combination with the intuition of unity. At this point, the two intuitions are functioning together as a third intuition: totality. A totality of mental impressions is an association of them within a mental extension—a unity.

However, such an association is not generally recognized as a totality. For it is a blend, in which individual mental impressions (generally apprehended as the qualities of a object) do not as a rule stand out in distinction. Some may do so when focused upon by the mind, but not all of them at once.

The Thinking Process

Rather, the multiple mental impressions compose properties, a multiple of which are in turn recognized as being combined in a totality. For individual properties of an object are apprehended as such even when they are not focused upon. It is also the case that a single quality can be recognized as a property. Thus there are individual mental impressions which are limited unities.

Whether these are combined in association to form a mental representation of a physical object, a mental image freely created by imagination, or the multiple imagery supporting a concept, they become either unities of mental impressions (a unity of unities), or, in the latter case, a unity of images (a unity of unities of unities). In each progressive case, individual units are combined into a totality of units.

The intuitions of unity and plurality function spontaneously in the recognition of mental impressions. For to apprehend them at all is to recognize them in this way. Then the intuitions of unity, plurality, and totality subsequently contribute to the formation of images. The latter is a first step in the imaginative process.

Concept formation, a further step, is also imaginative. But it is controlled by the understanding, the understanding being nothing more than a limiting act of imagination. Thus, because it is controlled, a concept is intellectual in character. It involves a careful selection of those properties which are to be made prominent in its function as a classification. The selected properties, represented by preexisting images, determine a definition. And the definition delimits the concept.

Consequently, a concept is a more thorough abstraction than an image. For there is an attempt to separate it from the relative spontaneity of experience and imagination. It is true that any image involves some degree of abstraction. But it is formed without precision, and generally without careful consideration as to how it is formed. Consequently, it is different than a concept. For a concept is crafted and precise. It is delimited by a definition, which makes it a classification. Thus it satisfies reason in its deliberate delineation of properties.

So the first intuition is an expression of focus. Focus is mental attention. Whether the mind focuses upon a single mental impression, or upon an entire field of mental impressions, it acts as the intuition of unity. In its focus upon one mental impression or a field of mental impressions, if either is being held in opposition to another of its kind, the mind's focus acts as an intuition of plurality. Furthermore, when it focuses upon an acknowledged plurality as a unity, it becomes the intuition of totality. These are all different ways of exercising focus and thus expressing unities.

When a field of focus is an association of mental impressions, it is a thought extension, which is an image. If physical experience is concerned, the images are recognized as representing physical objects or parts or properties of physical objects. Each object is characterized by being contiguous to and limited by another. But, in some cases, what appears to be an enclosed empty space will appear within the contiguous relations of physical objects. This is due to the properties of the objects, which influence their figure, or shape, creating gaps between the objects.

These spaces are not open. All, regardless of extent (be it millions of miles), are enclosed. For, when the limits of an enclosure cannot be detected, they must be assumed in order to satisfy the condition of unity. Hence the finitude of what might appear to be an infinite space. Since it is a collective

The Thinking Process

contiguity of extensions which constitutes space, any empty space exhibits the limited character of extension.

30. The Source of Mental Content

Material experience is an expression of universal consciousness. This consciousness, which is unlimited, transforms itself into an individual human awareness. Thus universal consciousness becomes self-limiting as to what it can experience. It is in this role that it furnishes the human mind with content. So it can be said that an individual person's experience of the material realm is a product of consciousness. But it is the product of a greater content of consciousness than his own.

Neither the representations of thought, nor the individual mental impressions constituting their qualities, resemble consciousness. Yet consciousness is the author of both. For it is the source of all mental impressions. Moreover, because these impressions are drawn from a realm of possibility, which is an unseen future, material experience is a dynamism. And dynamism involves change. Thus it is change which infuses meaning into experience. But it could not be recognized without thought.

Thought illustrates change by making it discernible to imagination and the intellect. And change exhibits spontaneity within the imagination, until the intellect brings it under causal relations. It is by means of making change meaningful in this way that the mind integrates material experience and draws it nearer to the unity of universal consciousness. Nevertheless, causal relations are not determinate. For their logical necessity cannot be demonstrated.

To recognize that universal consciousness can be self-limited, and that it produces material experience, is to acknowledge that material experience is an expression of the self-limitation of universal consciousness. But were it not for the intuitions, which arise from an exercise of mental focus, the mental impressions so received would remain confused and unarticulated. For they are prior to imagination and understanding.

The delineation of one mental impression and then another establishes their sequential flow. For to be recognized, they must come before the mind individually. This is, of course, prior to their combined representation in imagery. And, as their sequential appearance before the mind exhibits change, and thus facilitates a recognition of time, the changes are prior to a recognition of time.

Mental images, which appear to the mind as extensions of thought and physical experience, are finite because mental impressions are finite. For the images are composed of impressions. The impressions could not be gathered into associations if they were not finite. Consequently, they are. And what is finite stands in total dissociation from what is infinite. For there is but one infinite. Whereas there are many finites.

Not only are the individual elements of material experience finite, material experience as a whole is finite. For the latter is limited by the character of the former. And to be limited is to be finite. Therefore, since physical experience is expressed in terms of spatial relations, space is finite.

The Thinking Process

This is so, regardless of what the mind may wish to imagine. For, should it contradict reason, it could not advance without recognizing its own presumption. Finitude also applies to time, which is generated from changes in the relations of objects. Time is simply the order of this change.

Now finite entities can be delineated and defined. So, since material experience is composed of these, it is definable. But a definition is not active. Changes are active. Yet, if they are random, they have no meaning. So thought is needed to provide sequences of change with meaning. In other words, concepts are static. They are set in the mind like stones in a bracelet. They are laid out in a pattern. But the pattern is inert.

When change occurs, it disturbs the pattern like a kaleidoscope. So changes must be organized in the mind. For, where there are consistent relationships in the order of change, there is occasion for causal relations. And the consistency of these allows for prediction. When events may be predicted, they assume a purpose. They integrate the mind of the thinker with their flow. Thus material experience takes on meaning.

Events are held in the memory as something past and inalterable. This inertness of content characterizes the memory even while events under observation continue to progress. For what exist in memory are changes that have already occurred. They represent phenomena which are no longer undergoing change.

So memories are made up of independent images which do not change. Many of them support concepts that are set in a pattern of fixed relationships which previously had undergone change. Thus, insofar as the mind is concerned, memory is actualized experience. It is dead experience, experience of the past.

Beyond it, there is an anticipation of further changes: an openness to potential, which is merely felt. It cannot be understood. For this reason, no change can be registered in the mind, other than that which occurs within a train of thought. Therefore, given the static, and consequently determinate,[28] character of memory, it is thought alone which activates a comprehensive awareness of change. By means of the movement of thought, change is introduced to the human mind as a process. Thus it transforms the content of the mind into an expression of a dynamic within human consciousness.

Material change is limited in potential. In other words, though it is unlimited in possibility, it is limited in probability. This is to say that causal relations are probable relations. They cannot be necessary. Potentially anything might occur among them. But a consistent pattern of occurrence has been experienced. Consistency restricts potentiality. So it is in this way that experience moves anticipation into a narrowed sphere of expectancy.

This restriction is limited change. Thus material change is finite in character. It may ramify in many directions. But it may not do so indefinitely. Accordingly, the infinite has been translated into the finite. That is to say, material change brings about this translation insofar as it reduces the expectation of unlimited potential.

---

[28] It is determinate because there is no alteration in its character or relations.

The Thinking Process

Unlimited potential is infinite change. Moreover, it is instantaneous. It is a motion without progression. For there is no time to demark its motion. Time is demarcated by limited change—i.e., orderly change. Consequently, where there can be no recognition of sequence, there can be no progression.

When human understanding looks for an explanation of unlimited potential, it cannot determine whether it is a process, or whether it should be considered a foundation for process. The mind asks: Is universal consciousness active in its potential, the activity being incomprehensible?

Or is its potential at rest, becoming active only in its material expression? Reason is led to this conundrum because it is limited to considerations of activity and rest. But these are human concepts. And, as such, they cannot be applied to universal consciousness, except by way of metaphor.

Nevertheless, however limited in comparison to universal consciousness the transitions of human thought may be, they do reflect its operations through their exhibition of a process of becoming. In other words, they reflect the operations of universal consciousness through their transition by means of change from what is potential to what is actual.

For the actual in the material domain is grounded in the potential. And the potential is the activity of universal consciousness. That is to say, the actual, which is an expression of the potential, is made present to human awareness by consciousness. This transition by means of change is the process of one differentiated thought succeeding another. It is also the process of a physical object changing in character or location.

Thus a sequence of thoughts creates an awareness of change in the human mind by means of such transitions. The awareness results from an experience of one image or concept following another in the mind: one thought with a particular content succeeding another which had a different content. In this way, it is the process of thinking which registers change before the mind.

This content of consciousness which is processed through thought is the only part of human experience which can be articulated. It alone can be known. To human beings, it is known as the world. For the world is all that is accessible to imagination and intellect. It is all that is known by the thinking mind. On the other hand, there is universal consciousness. Universal consciousness is reflected in human consciousness when the latter is considered without reference to its material content. It can only be experienced as consciousness. It cannot be known by the mind.

Conversely, individual mental impressions constitute feelings. When they are of a character to be independent of associations as qualities in objects, emotions can arise from sequences of them. Otherwise, they constitute objects represented by thoughts. Thus only feelings, emotions, and thoughts are apprehended by the mind. They are the realm of the material. Consequently, insofar as human understanding is concerned, the world is material. And only thoughts about it can be understood.

Since associated mental impressions constitute objects of thought, they are not only experienced, as is the case with consciousness, independent feelings, and emotions. They are articulated for human understanding. Whereas consciousness, independent feelings, and emotions are not.

Mental impressions recognized as qualities of physical objects are generally thought of as provided by the senses.

The Thinking Process

But they are known only in the mind. It is these impressions which supply material for the images and concepts of physical representation. By means of them, the mind recognizes a world which is external to it.

So for human awareness, extensions composed of associated mental impressions, be they physical objects or objects of thought, constitute the articulation of experience. Along with feelings and emotions, they are the world. And consciousness alone does not appear to be such a world.

The world appears orderly and determined to human awareness. For material change is orderly. It is organized by the intellect into a proportional shifting of relations, which can be systemized in thought. But any system, in virtue of its ordered relations, suggests a greater degree of determinism than freedom. Thus material change only haltingly suggests a free and dynamic character. It does not achieve it. Conversely, in universal consciousness all is potential. For its ground of change can neither be conceived nor imagined by the human mind.

Human thought is a hybrid function. It is hybrid because the content of consciousness is material and consciousness is not. Yet it is consciousness which delivers mental impressions to the mind. And it is consciousness, in its exercise of focus and attention, which forms the mental impressions into image representations, and these into experience.

But what is consciousness? Other than to speak of it as an indeterminate realm of potential—that from which mental impressions and changes among them originate—it cannot be known. Consciousness is experienced by human awareness, which awareness is that consciousness. Thus human awareness is consciousness experiencing itself. No more can be said of it, but that in human experience it is a self-limiting condition. The limitation imposed is that of limited experience.

Therefore, being characterized by limited experience, human awareness exhibits a restricted capacity for a recognition of the potential for change. Moreover, though it is self-limiting as to content, consciousness itself is not limited. Consciousness cannot be attributed to its content as a datum. Rather, the data of consciousness, which are characterized by a condition of finitude, are single mental impressions or associations of impressions.

Though a single mental impression is not an extension, it is recognized by the mind as finite. For it is individually distinguishable. And it exhibits duration. In other words, any one mental impression is individually and temporally differentiated from other mental impressions. But it is unextended. Extension, be it physical or an object of thought, arises from associations of mental impressions.

Thus, since they are finite, single mental impressions and associations of mental impressions are contained within a consciousness which, being self-limited as to experience in this way, articulates only limited representations to itself. These finite entities are all that is contained within the experience of human consciousness, other than the experience of itself.

The Thinking Process

31. Feelings and Emotions

Feelings and emotions are part of the content of consciousness. But they are not thought extensions. Feelings are single mental impressions. And emotions arise from a series of these, which function as independent elements of the emotion. Thus neither are held before the mind as images.

For no thought extension is composed of a single mental impression, as is the case with an individual feeling or the separate components of an emotion. Moreover, any image references qualities found in physical objects. Thus associated mental impressions are, either directly or through imaginative reconstruction, representative of the qualities of physical objects.

Now, like thought, memory only registers images and concepts. Consequently, feelings and emotions are neither thought nor represented in memory in the manner in which they were initially experienced. For this reason, when they are reintroduced to the mind after an initial experience, they must be represented by images connected with that experience. And the images must represent something other than the feeling or emotion.

So, given that feelings and emotions are expressed in memory by thought extensions which do not directly represent them, they are only prefigured by images. Because these images must represent what cannot be directly held in memory or in a thought, they are not derived from the feelings or emotions themselves. Rather, they are composed of the physical circumstances, thoughts, and behavior which originally accompanied the feelings or emotions when they were experienced. These are what are held in memory and recalled before the mind.

32. The Representation of Consciousness

Since consciousness is neither bound, extended, nor divisible, it cannot be articulated. For these are the properties of finitude. And they are missing from consciousness. So together they form a concept of negation, expressing what consciousness is not. There is no positive representation.

As an experience like no other, consciousness can be imagined to submit to division and a momentary expansion, or extension, only in the sense that water submits to the insertion of a harpoon. It fleetingly moves away from the harpoon, closing behind it, obliterating its effect. Hence the peculiar observation that one indivisible consciousness embraces many enclosed states of mind. For consciousness is divided in content, but not in itself. The condition of a division in content alone creates the sense of an enclosure and isolation of a state of mind, or even of the overall awareness of an individual person, which person entertains multiple states of mind.

For this reason, a yawning gulf in human understanding is revealed. The mind cannot conceive an indistinguishable unity in which each individual consciousness is an expression of the same single consciousness. Nor can it account for the manner in which individual states of mind collectively represent one person. It also cannot conceive a connection between consciousness and the content of consciousness.

Moreover, an individual consciousness is that in which the data of physical experience are represented, but in which the whole of that experience is not contained, as causal relations would suggest. This leads to a conviction that the physical world is separate from the mind. Such a dichotomy brings about the illusion of a thing-in-itself, which suggests a physical realm independent of consciousness.

Nevertheless, all things are a product of consciousness, however occult the agency of their presentation. If an individual should examine his experience, he will see that he can only know the world through his mind. Moreover, that world submits to his understanding. It is what he can articulate directly or indirectly in thought.

Conversely, he knows consciousness only as immediate experience. It cannot be conceived. For it is not finite and cannot be a content of his awareness which would submit to intellectual analysis. Thus consciousness is experienced as being in the world but not of it. Yet a person will declare that he is a conscious being. And, in doing so, he has a definite sense of what he means, though it is beyond articulation.

33. Higher Thought

The rise of humanity is said to have begun with tools. Thus the development of increasingly complex civilization may be considered to have involved the internalization of tools, as well as the internalization of the phenomena with which they are concerned. For example, mathematics is a systematic, internalized set of tools designed for dealing with equally internalized aspects of nature. Nature becomes internalized because physical experience must be conceptualized to be intellectually understood.

There is an integration of the internalized material. For it must be systemized to create the relations which make it useful. Such an internal organization may be increasingly enlarged. It is in this manner that mathematics aids science, particularly physical science. It supplies it with proportional relations. And science aids the further development of itself through continued investigation and organization.

The tool, mathematics, is itself a science. For it too has a history of development. Thus the concept of the triangle arose and has proven to be a cornerstone of geometry. Geometry in turn has become a building block of physical science, especially prior to the development of mathematical analysis.

Apparently, a rough concept of the triangle was developed to aid in the measurement of agricultural fields in Egypt . And it is alleged that the Greeks borrowed it from the Egyptians and created mathematics as an abstract discipline.[29] Using this tool, the fertile seeds of physical science were subsequently planted by Aristarchus of Samos, Hipparchus, Archimedes, Ptolemy, Galileo, Kepler, and Newton.

The mathematical discipline grew at an accelerated pace through the seventeenth, eighteenth, and nineteenth centuries. Physical science also flourished in richness of detail and

---

[29] Sir Thomas L. Heath, *A Manual of Greek Mathematics*.

The Thinking Process

relation, utilizing mathematical tools to integrate its relations. Other sciences were added, each using mathematics in varying degree.

Regardless of how much mathematics was employed by each, all the sciences used the same logical methods of investigation and organization which had been modeled for them by Euclid's *Elements*. In the twentieth century, Einstein and others applied the mathematics they had inherited to a reinterpretation of the physical relations of physical science. Thus the process continues.

From this remarkable, ongoing internalization and development of tools, as well as the internalization and integration of the experiences to which the tools were applied, have come many other fields of human endeavor. Philosophy, literature, art, and religion have been internalized and organized by means of tools which are different from those described.

They have been systemized in varying degree. So humanity progresses by an internal encompassment of external experience. Not only are various departments of experience developed into separate fields of knowledge and representation. They are brought together in one vast organ of civilization.

It is in this manner that material experience is continually modified and integrated into the mind. Mind is the instrument of consciousness. It is increasingly universal in all but its rational limitations. Its recognized and integrated relations of change suggest, without achieving, the open-ended, unlimited potential of universal consciousness.

Thus the mind is drawn toward freedom, or lack of limitation. Its increasing encompassment and integration of experience defy the apparent limitations of the material realm. They signify possibility. For, were it not for the accessibility of potential, such a feat of unification could not occur. Thus humankind is ever progressing in the direction of universal consciousness.

Universal consciousness is unlimited potential. Reason, on the other hand, is an instrument of material limitation, classifying and relating experience according to finite limits. But it acts as a bridge between mind and universal consciousness, drawing into the unifying character of the former what had seemed alien to it in the latter.

34. Three Brief Topics

(1) *Metaphorical Thinking*: Deductive reasoning, particularly when considered in its syllogistic form, exhibits an evident association of terms, as when the middle terms of two premises join the remaining subject and predicate in a conclusion. But metaphorical thinking is different. It might be likened to images freely rotating in the mind, briefly facing one another at diverse points. By means of this process, a number of disparate properties are momentarily associated.

If any of these temporary bonds should hold, and a meaningful linking of images develops within an enlarged context, then a bridge is made. And a transition of thought runs across it. For example, take the couplet by Alexander Pope inscribed on the collar of the king's dog:

The Thinking Process

> I am his Highness' dog at Kew
> Pray tell me, sir, whose dog are you.[30]

Through a repetition of the word "dog" in both lines, the poem associates the reader of the couplet with the wearer of the collar. This association is based on the assumption that the dog might think people are dogs as well as himself and find nothing offensive in it.

For a moment, a simple association is established between two very different references: the one to a dog, the other to a human being understood as a dog. The couplet induces the reader into accepting the association. This results in a broadened range of meaning for the dog image. It becomes a metaphor.

But an insult is thus conveyed to the reader because she does not regard dogs and people as on the same level. It is in this way that a few properties from two disparate images are wrenched into association, forming, from the point of view of the reader of the couplet, an unhappy marriage of images.

(2) *Reason Seeks Simplicity*: In science there is no absolute truth. But that does not matter. For it is not necessary that a scientific theory be true to be effective. It need only gather the greatest amount of experimentally verifiable data under the least complex set of relations. When more data is gathered under a modification of the theory, and the modified theory exhibits a system of fewer and less complex relations, then the new theory will replace the old.

---

[30] Alexander Pope, "Engraved on the Collar of a Dog, Which I Gave to His Royal Highness."

(3) *Simplicity of Thought*: Truth is simple, while convoluted explanations are a sign of confusion, pretension, a concealment of intellectual weakness, or untruth. Look anywhere. And it will be seen that this is so. For example, religions which become mired in symbolism sacrifice the elemental force of their insights.

Or a work of art, encrusted with a labored symbolism or ostentatious technique, obscures the effect of its subtler relations. And there is science. Was it not the greater simplicity of Copernicus' explanation of the movements of heavenly bodies that revolutionized celestial mechanics?

35. Mental Focus

The mind has a narrow range of focus. For example, let a person envision three apples on a shelf. When she tries to focus upon all of them at once, she cannot do so. If she tries to compare the two apples on the left with the one on the right, her mind will move back and forth between them.

So let it be assumed that she focuses on two apples. The image is vague. Therefore, to sharpen it, she narrows her attention to the contiguous parts of the apples. She finds that she can observe the parts with greater precision, though some details will remain obscure. This is the best she can do, beyond narrowing her focus to one part of one apple, thus picking up previously unobserved details by means of a close examination.

The Thinking Process

The point is that a person cannot see two complete, contiguous apples without sacrificing detail. It is uncertain that she can visualize them as more than colored shapes. Even then, the shapes will involve little more than general impressions of roundness. Moreover, the color, though recognized according to hue, is indistinct in variation of tone. Beyond this, there is an inability of her mind to grasp them whole.

More importantly, what she certainly cannot do is visualize three apples simultaneously. To visualize them, her focus must shift from one to another then another. Or her attention will move from two to the other. In this case, there are few details of the first two, which are bound together as one in her mind. She moves from these to an examination of the third apple.

It is true that three apples together can make a collective impression when she encounters them in experience. But it is their general quantity and shape which will impress her. And even these details will be arrived at in a rapid succession of separate views. So long as the three apples are regarded collectively, they will remain largely unarticulated in her mind. That is, the majority of qualities or properties constituting their makeup will be unaccounted for.

But she must have a sense of what she is about. So, to compensate for the initial impressions, since they are based upon shape and color recognition alone, her mind will draw an image of an apple from memory. In this way, she will guess that this is what she has encountered in triplicate. Thus the original apples will remain unarticulated until her mind hones in for a closer inspection, singling out one apple or two at the most, then focusing in further to gather local details.

So how do acts of comparison occur? Mental attention narrows any set of details to a comparison of pairs. First two details are compared. Then these two together are set against another. And the same is done with a fourth detail, etc. What does this indicate? It demonstrates that the mind entertains one comparison at a time.

This act of comparison may be called a division. For a comparison involves a partition of one into two. Or, if not this, then it involves two things brought into a proximity to one another, which is a division between them. Any previously observed details are experienced as shadows of suggestion, held in abeyance in the mind until they can be brought forward for further examination.

Thus, in the case of any pair of details, a single comparison is being made. Initially the mind entertains a detail from a proximate portion of, say, each of two apples. It might be the curves of their adjacent sides. Then another set of details, like a difference in textures, is examined. While this proceeds, each previous comparison is held in mental abeyance, where it lies faded out of focus. For only an examination of a pair of individual details can be held under mental focus at one time. Following any initial comparison, another set of details can then be observed, then another, in ongoing succession.

What about the intuition of unity, since this philosophy places it at the origin of mental articulation? Clearly, it is this intuition which is exercised in the act of mental focus. For the intuition of unity articulates a field of focus, however narrow. And it is the variability of mental focus which provides the sense of limitation.

The Thinking Process

So what role do these play in the examination of detail? The examination of detail is the means the mind employs in making a comparison. And without the intuition of unity, which is an exercise of mental focus, a recognition and comparison of details would not be possible. For the details are either qualities or properties, which are respectively individual or composite unities.

There is, of course, a unity of consciousness which makes possible the intuition of unity and its application by means of mental focus. But the unity of consciousness is a unity without bounds or division—i.e., it does not exhibit limits. So what establishes those limits is the intuition of unity, which is a limiting focus of conscious awareness.

In other words, consciousness places its attention upon a limited field of mental impressions. Because this application of attention is carried out within the unity of consciousness, whose field of observation is thus narrowed, its result is a limited unity. The recognition of this unity as limited converts the first intuition into the second, which is the intuition of plurality. For the recognition of limitation involves a comparison of separate unities.

So necessary is the employment of focus that, should a person recall an apple from memory, she would need to do it under the intuition of unity. And she could only do so initially by means of a vague image. For she could not clearly visualize much detail. A sense of shape might be the only detail suggesting the whole, until other details like color are consecutively added. Thus, subsequent to the initial recall, she would begin to augment the image with added details.

Consequently, any attempt at an accumulation of detail would require a fundamental division into two parts which constitutes a comparison. For three details compared would require two consecutive acts of comparison. Clarity would demand that a single detail at a time be opposed to another, and that consecutively examined details constitute a more extensive articulation.

It is in this way that a person either encounters or remembers an apple. She may choose to examine or recall a blemished apple. The blemish constitutes her initial focus. It then suffices to provide a foundation for a fuller mental representation of the apple, as more details are subsequently added. For the full representation cannot begin all at once, even when the object is being drawn from memory.

Or, since the person is able to shift the breadth of her observation—focusing in or focusing out—she might withdraw her attention from a multi-detailed examination of the apple, choosing to focus on one detail, a blemish, at the expense of allowing an indistinct generality of the other details to be formed in her mind.

That generality might be limited to an emphasis on the apple's shape or color. In any case, regardless of what is held in abeyance in her mind and what is brought into comparison, the fact that there is a required individual selection of paired details for making any comparison demonstrates how narrow the range of mental focus truly is.

36. Relationship

As stated in the previous chapter, the mind can only clearly apprehend a relationship between two entities. If the relationship is between a greater number of entities, it will not be imagined in any detail. So, if three qualities, like the color, gloss, and solidity of a brass rod, are considered individually, one in comparison to another, they are clearly distinguishable. But, if the three are held in simultaneous association in the mind, they blend and form an extension: an object. Thus they are inseparable from the extension which they compose. For it is the object which is considered. And its individual qualities are subordinate to it.

So, in addition to the fact that the apprehension of the combined qualities of an object is unclear in detail, if three objects—say a brass rod, a glass window pane, and a wooden sill—are considered at once, they can only be represented together by the imagination in the vaguest terms. For, when three or more objects are visualized together, they not only appear indistinctly in themselves, but in their relationship to one another. To achieve distinction, they must be apprehended in pairs. And to arrive at exactness of detail, this must be broken down to an individual comparison of qualities or properties.

Again, as stated in the previous chapter, to represent three objects, the imagination must relate two of them, then add a third. When the third is placed in a relationship with the two others, it is, in effect, being related to a combined unit. In other words, as mental focus shifts from an initial relationship between two objects to a relationship of the two of them considered together in comparison to a third, the first two, being united, become one entity for the subsequent relation.

Thus an iterative process is developed. It is a thought sequence. Two objects are brought together in one thought by means of mental focus. Then, in another thought, mental attention shifts, leaving the first two objects in combination while removing its focus from the relationship between them. When a third object is brought into comparison with the first two, whose relationship is already established, the situation is treated by the mind as one entity being related to one entity.

The process continues with the addition of each new member to the combined relationship. Thus a fourth object is related in the same manner to the first three. The first three are treated by the mind as a single entity in relationship with the fourth. In this way, any new relationship is always treated as a comparison of two.

All representations combining more than two things are presented to the imagination in an unfocused manner. It is as though the mind were reviewing them in passing, failing to note individual details which would establish a relationship between them. If it were to pause at such details, the selected details would be rendered as though contiguous to one another. This would involve two of them at a time and no more. For a comparison can only focus upon a contiguity of two.

Consequently, it is not possible to simultaneously focus upon a relationship of two entities and observe their relationship to a void. For this would involve three entities in two separate relationships. Initially there would be one entity and

The Thinking Process

the other entity. Then both these entities registered in the mind as one would be considered in relation to the void. Thus, there are two relationships. And each relationship would require a separate act of mental focus to establish it. So they must be done in sequence. Accordingly, it can be seen that the number of relationships which is dealt with in one mental act is always one.

Yet, not only can the imagination not apprehend a relationship when it involves an attempted focus on more than two details. It cannot apprehend a single detail alone. For the absence of a relationship between two entities cannot be apprehended at all. Any entity which is represented to the mind is always placed against another by way of comparison. This is because a single entity must be divided in the mind into at least two comparative features to be visualized, as when a shape or color is seen to vary.

It is not possible to visualize shape alone without a variation in contour. Even a Euclidean line, when drawn, must exhibit the character of a thin rectangle with distinct sides to give it visible breadth. And a monotone color could not be imagined alone. Whereas, if the color varied, it could. This is the visualizing process. An image, as an object of thought, must have multiple qualities. Regardless of the type of representation, the situation remains the same.

This is so even if the entity must be considered against a void. The void becomes an entity for this purpose. It completes the unity required of an object of thought by acting as a spatial background in establishing a relationship between it and the entity of interest. A *finite* unity is always established when a thought represents one entity in opposition to another.

For it is in this way that the mutually delimiting entity and void together create a unity which is finite in character. The finite unity of interest is the entity. The void delimits it. It is as though the entity, be it object or detail, were drawn as a figure on a board. The part of the board outside the figure gives shape to the figure.

37. Six Topics

(1) *Instinct and Mental Freedom*: Instinct is often viewed as the hard-wiring of a specific pattern of behavior. But it can be more liberally understood as an inclination toward a particular orientation of behavior. This would be a tendency, psychological and emotional in origin, exhibiting a less than rigid character. So, if instinct is a tendency, it should be further asked, what is the nature of animal awareness? Can animals make associations which determine their behavior without having to reason?

In fact, do human beings do what they do strictly by means of imagination and reason? Imagination and reason are tools which are useful but limited in function. So, given their general but less than universal employment, should they be held as the only factors in a consideration of the character of a human being? These questions are important at a practical level. For, if instinct is simply an emotional memory—a trigger activated by releasers in the environment—then it cannot be overridden. But an animal does not always follow its instincts.

The Thinking Process

Nor are human beings unmotivated by instincts. There is the example of a woman unconsciously adjusting her hair in the presence of an attractive man, thus displaying her breasts. And there is the example of a man absentmindedly stretching in the presence of an attractive woman, thus displaying his pectorals. Other such subtle behaviors can be noted. But, because a human being lives within a closed shell of self, that person may not see the effects of personal instinct on behavior.

So instinct, though widely applicable, is limited and variable. It is a product of nature, made for specific practical uses and not for others. In lower forms of sentient life it is dominant. But it is not absolute. And, conversely, though human beings think, this does not mean they do not sometimes act out of instinct. What it does mean is that they should not invest hubris in imagination or reason. They should respect their use, since they are largely compelled to live by them. They can hardly do otherwise. But to live by imagination and reason is to know their limits.

(2) *Logic, Nature, and Consciousness*: Logic is grounded in the way human beings think. It has a causal parallel in nature because human beings, when considered in strictly material terms, are products of nature. But the human intellect, as a derivative of nature, is more limited than nature is. Consequently, thinking does not conceive all there is in nature.

Paradoxically, human beings can transcend nature. As conscious beings with a capacity for imagination and rational thought, they have developed a conceptual apprehension of their experience of consciousness. As any concept describing consciousness is negative (describing what it is not), it is indirect. So it is unsatisfactory. But, in spite of this limitation, a person can recognize that consciousness is the ground from which material nature springs. For it is the only means by which material nature is known.

(3) *Material Analysis*: If a human being were not conceived as an expression of material being, but as an expression of spirit (i.e., as a disembodied soul), would she be subject to a different set of limitations, as Thomas Aquinas would have it?[31] This question cannot be entertained, so long as a material analysis of the content of consciousness is considered a greater approach to truth than the miracle of consciousness itself.

(4) *Reason and Civilization*: What faculty of understanding does the mind possess other than reason? A person may experience consciousness directly. But he can say nothing about it, unless he ventures to use reason. Thus a work of art or a mystical experience may be experienced. But it cannot become an object of discourse without reason. Reason is the author of civilization, though much may lay beyond reason's reach.

(5) *The Uncertainty of Fact*: The conceptual faculty of a human being allows her to gather up a working knowledge of nature. This faculty is classification. It produces facts. But classification can cut in many directions across material experience, lending a variable character to facts. So, since they

---

[31] St. Thomas Aquinas, "On Being and Essence."

partake both of experience and the way human beings classify it, facts do not constitute a ground for truth. Experience alone is the ground.

(6) *Order and Chaos*: Insofar as any human being is aware, there is no such thing as chaos. Order is the only reality the mind can conceive. For, if there were such a thing as chaos, the human intellect could not embrace it. A person might attempt to imagine the explosion of a bomb into fragments. But any attempt to depict the scattering of parts must place them in relation to one another. That relation is order, not chaos.

38. Five Topics

(1) *The Organizing Mind*: An anomaly is that which does not accord with the contemporary conception of things. Were an iron ax head to float, people would be amazed. But if ax heads had always been known to float and this fact had long since been incorporated into humankind's reasoning, people would be no less surprised to see one sink. What matters is the organization of the mind. What that organization might be is subordinated to the task of making observations fit logically together.

(2) *Conceptual Interdependence*: All concepts are interdependent. Except by a process of deliberate omission, the human mind could not conceive one thing without conceiv-

ing others. For the latter are instrumental in filling out a conception of the former. If a person were to encounter a chair for the first time where there were no other bodies, not even the body of the observer, how would she conceive the chair? Determining its size without a standard of comparison would be impossible. The shape would appear indistinct and confused. And, as for its purpose, the body of the observer being unknown, the purpose would be meaningless.

(3) *Imagination and Reason*: Most thinking is not rational. It is imaginative, employing a series of associated images. Originating from encounters with physical properties and stored in memory, images are associated with one another in varying degrees by means of the properties contained in each of them. A series of such associations may make it possible to recognize an activity and suggest a movement of the will. It is frequently only after this has been achieved by means of imagination, that the mind subsequently conceptualizes and logically organizes its thought.

As a rule, extensive deliberation following the conversion of images to concepts does not occur. For it is not at the time of the formation of the concepts, but only after having drawn them from memory, that the mind is prepared to organize them into a logical structure. However, an occasional exception is made when new concepts are formed from imagination to fill gaps in a logical structure. Nevertheless, the final result is often the creation of an illusion that the entire thought process was rational.

Thus a deception arises. For thought is motivated by fine nuances of feeling. As images are closer to experience, feelings are more intimately associated with them than with

The Thinking Process

concepts. But, since logical order exhibits greater control, the mind seeks it to justify its activity. For control is a great motivator. And the desire for it is felt.

In pursuit of logical order, people capitalize on simple statements of reason by integrating them into systems of thought. It is in this way that conceptual thinking has become the backbone of culture. For it can be clearly understood without the troubling interference of emotional nuance.

Thus it is easy to pass on and preserve. But the creative portion of the process only occurs when images are being associated, and when concepts are spontaneously formed from images to fill gaps in reasoning. It does not occur when concepts are borrowed from memory and given a logical order.

In sum, what this amounts to is that a person can have a lot of insight. But he cannot act upon it extensively and consistently without a buildup of the logical and systematic organization of the insights. This is the gift which reason bestows upon imagination. Yet it remains greatly inferior to it in inventive power.

(4) *Science and Philosophy*: Reason is a product of nature. But what is nature a product of? Can its origin be uncovered by reason? Origin of process is not the question here. Origin of existence is the question. Reason can map nature with increasing precision and practical utility. But it cannot measure the depths of it. It cannot go beyond its own limits. This suggests that science represents an ongoing adjustment of humanity to its experience. But the adjustment is not a full explanation.

Imagination can transcend the evidence of reason and sense. But, in so doing, it cannot demonstrate any of its speculations beyond those two faculties. So it lacks assurance. Nevertheless, much of human experience defies empirical demonstration. This is so even within science. For much of science is speculative, in spite of observational assurances. So the mind cannot be satisfied with demonstrations alone. It must speculate. But what it provides is a shadow, though it is a very important and necessary shadow.

(5) *Nothingness Is Inconceivable*: Nothingness is inconceivable because all concepts are supported by imagery which is composed of mental impressions. And there are no impressions of nothing. So no image, and therefore no concept, of nothingness can be formed in the mind. The accustomed concept of nothingness is simply a negative description of something which no longer is or of something which is assumed to have never been.

39. Arithmetic and Verbal Logic

Quantities can be verbally expressed. But an arithmetical statement is not the same as a statement in verbal discourse. For the conceptualizations of arithmetical statements concern number. And number is limited in terms of a simple form of differentiation of one from another. Numbers are determined by multiples of units. And these units do not differ in charac-

The Thinking Process

ter, other than that of a magnitude determined by context, such as is exemplified by the varied roles of the unit 1 in ¼ and 10.

Thus multiplicity pertains to the function of arithmetical units. And these units, considered simply as units, have few properties other than the fact that they are units. Numbers are expressive of a variant multiplicity in relation to them. For the arithmetical unit establishes relations of proportion between rational numbers.

Accordingly, it can be seen that verbal reasoning and arithmetical reasoning are not the same in reference. Verbal logic works with an extended range of associations which is much broader than that of arithmetic. The extended range is achieved on the basis of a wide variety of properties shared between the subjects and predicates of statements, and in the way these properties are shared.

In protracted chains of reason, operations can be carried out upon the basis of a family of broadly associated properties. It is in this way that thinking advances by means of a varied association of properties. For different concepts may enter a train of thought, the new ones introducing new properties, thereby enlarging the range of thought. Thus there is an integrated shifting of the process, where the train of thought may even move to another string of associations altogether, a new property being drawn from the last concept under consideration.

So it can be seen that there is an unlimited plenitude of properties in verbal discourse. For it is a field as broad as experience itself and not limited to a narrow sphere of concepts based on a few properties, like multiples of units. So, whereas the parameters of arithmetical reasoning are restricted, the materials of verbal association are unlimited.

40. Mathematical and Verbal Discourse

There must be rules of transformation in verbal discourse, just as there are in mathematics. But the rules in verbal discourse are fewer than those in mathematics. And, while logical rules may be held to underlie mathematical rules, they do so only in the sense that the narrow range of associations in mathematics are associations which can be logically understood.

In any case, there must be rules of transformation in both forms of reasoning. For both involve conceptual transitions in thought. And, unlike imaginative images, concepts are inflexible, be they verbal or mathematical. As concepts, they are defined. In other words, they are closed, rather than open like imaginative images.

Their properties are precisely determined. So their internal meaning cannot be altered in the way it can in a comparison of images. Because of this, associations between concepts cannot be turned about in the mind, as images are when their properties are being momentarily aligned in rough comparisons.

In the matter of concepts, the mind must proceed diligently with astringency of purpose, carefully recognizing matches of properties between concepts, or assuming them where not observed. For these properties are determined by

The Thinking Process

definition. Or, if not, they are assumed to do so by means of the predication of one concept upon another, in which the subject of a statement takes on properties its definition does not specify. In either case, the concepts themselves cannot be internally altered in any way.

For this reason, the concepts embedded in propositional statements are consistently recognized to be neither more nor less than what they are. So the mind must establish associations between them, including additions of meaning, without violating the integrity of their properties. For they cannot be handled in loose fashion.

They must remain inviolate for the sake of clarity in discourse. Thus any augmentation of properties regarding a concept must be passed on from thought to thought by external means, as when the property "white" is carried forward among the following statements.

> *White* houses are houses which are cool in summer.
> Some houses are *white* houses.
> Therefore, some houses are houses which are cool in summer.

"White" is an adjective appended to the concept "houses." So in neither premise is the concept house internally altered.

Now, if the question should arise as to how any new insight might occur, the answer must be that imagination enters the thought process with its free play of imagery. The resulting imagery is then translated into a concept. In this way, a new concept enters the chain of reason. But this is the exception which makes the reasoning process creative and original. What is generally being done is logic.

Logic is the norm of the reasoning process. For it is the skeleton to which the flesh of imagination is fastened. Logical forms and their transitions are systematic. They are the greater part of the reasoning process. For insights are few. It is logic which drives discourse. Its systematic and consistent character makes it predictable. That is its advantage. For it may be checked for error. This renders it intellectually trustworthy.

The logical character of a syllogistic proposition is determined through a relation of predicate to subject. The association of the predicate with the subject resembles the implication of a conditional statement in that it indicates that one thing must follow upon the presence of another. If the statement is, "white houses are cool in summer," it may be restated as, "if it is a white house, then it is cool in summer." Both statements involve associations which transfer a property—cool in summer—either from predicate to subject, or from consequent to antecedent. Affirm the subject. And the predicate is implied. Or, affirm the antecedent. And the consequent is implied.

The forms of logic are structured, which means they can be expressed in symbolic terms without consideration of the specific character of the concepts involved. Until the terms are defined, the statements do not make a reference to experience. So logical form does not determine empirical truth. Insofar as it alone is concerned, only the correct positioning of the terms within a proper structure matters. It is in this formal sense that the transformation rules of logic resemble the transformation rules of mathematics and may be understood to be interchangeable with them.

The Thinking Process

In verbal expression the rules are more restricted in variety than they are in mathematics. But verbal expression is greater in its associations of properties because it reflects the whole of experience. Whereas arithmetic (for example) functions narrowly, due to its restriction of fundamental properties to units and a multiplicity of units.

This restriction allows for extended chains of reckoning which are more easily made long and complex, as exemplified in algebraic expression (but which is no less so in geometrical reasoning). Thus, since the fundamental properties of arithmetic are restricted to units and multiples of units, many cross-references are put into effect in ingenious ways. So mathematics does complex things with very simple materials. Thus it can only be said to be associative in a severely limited degree insofar as properties are concerned.

In spite of the logical formality of reason in general (verbal or mathematical), the relations it forms are associative. They are a matter of the association of concepts by means of properties. But, whereas associations between imaginative images are free, associations between concepts are definitionally bound.

One concept must be associated with another specifically in terms of the properties pointed up by the definitions of the two concepts. Or one concept must be externally modified in terms of another by means of predication. A statement like "all dogs are mammals" is an example of the former. And a statement such as "dogs are smooth talkers" is an example of the latter. Employing the latter statement in the following way,

Smooth talkers are deceitful.

> Dogs are smooth talkers.
> Therefore, dogs are deceitful.

it can be seen how the concept "dogs," having been externally modified by "smooth talkers," is carried forward in reason.

In contrast with this, the most obscure feature of an imaginative image may be singled out for the sake of its association with another image. Such a feature would not be a definitional property because images do not have definitions. Thus, though they do have properties, they are not bound to them as fixed. Whereas concepts are classifications, each of whose definitional properties is supported by fixed imagery.

This imagery can be conceptualized, or rendered into a subclassification. Thus the two units which constitute the number 2 are subclassifications of a more inclusive classification. They are concepts supporting another concept, the number 2. This means that supporting properties are supported by properties. Such a process could proceed ad infinitum were it not that it is terminated by the limitations of the mind.

Nonetheless, however constrained by definitions the imaginative process may appear to be in reasoning, and whatever may be the greater flexibility of the same process in its relating of free images, the two processes are united by a single function of the mind, which is association. Thus the relations of reason are associative, just as are the relations of imagination.

Rational numbers are concepts which are rendered associative with one another because they have a commensurate

The Thinking Process

property. That property is the arithmetical unit 1. It is an extension without a reference to limits. For it has no size. It has only magnitude within a specific context. Rational numbers, be they whole or fraction, are composed of such units. Irrational numbers are approximations of rational numbers. Thus all numbers are associative, though the later are so only by suggestion. This means numbers can be compared in terms of their units, which are their properties. So logical relations between them can be established.

Mathematical transformations involve ratio relations between quantities or between segments of lines or curves. When an irrational number (or an incommensurate line) enters into a computation or comparison with a rational number (or a commensurate line), an incommensurate relationship is established as a non-ratio. So it stands in the relation of image to concept. The image, which is the irrational, is not defined. So its exact relationship to the concept cannot be determined. For the concept is a classification with regulated properties. And the image is not.

An extended explication would demonstrate the role of ratios in all rational arithmetical operations. Ratios apply to geometrical relations as well, with the exception of incommensurables, which are the equivalent of irrational numbers. But even irrational numbers ultimately submit to the rule of ratios. Though they do so, as it were, unwillingly. For they stand in the imperfect relationship of an image to a concept. In other words, an irrational number remains an unclassified image, while a rational number is a concept.

As to numbers in particular, if a number is indeterminate in both character and function, it is transcendental, or not definitively related to any other number. Thus its lack of definitiveness must be tolerated in mathematical operations. This practice is permitted on the assumption that irrational numbers have limits.

In other words, it is observed that they are defined ever more precisely as their digital representation is extended. Each digit of that extension reduces the margin of inexactness and increases the number's definitiveness. Nevertheless, irrational numbers are never defined exactly. So they are never truly mathematical concepts.

Incommensurate quantities like these occur in plenitude because experience prior to conceptualization is inherently indeterminate. Since mathematics cannot incorporate the whole of experience within its conceptual framework—i.e., within the domain of its rational numbers—much of that experience is left indeterminate. But the appearance of indeterminate elements results in a need for their accommodation as incommensurate or irrational. Thus the transformation rules, which are created for the sake of defined concepts, must at times be used to process elements which are not.

Arithmetic differs from language in being more flexible by rule and more constrained in properties. For the arithmetical unit is the fundamental property in arithmetical operations, a number being a cumulative integration of units. Ratio is the fundamental axiom. Geometry likewise operates on the basis of a point, a line being a cumulative integration of points. And ratio, as exhibited in Euclid's common notions, is the fundamental axiom of geometry as well.

So the principle of ratio is that from which the rules of mathematical transformation are derived. And these are numerous. For a paucity in properties demands greater

The Thinking Process

flexibility in their manipulation by rule. Logical transformations in language, on the other hand, require fewer rules, since the properties of language are limited only by the range of human experience.

The fundamental axiom of language is association, from which the relations of similarity and difference are determined. This is not unlike ratio, which is quantitative association. So the general rules of logic are derived from two axioms: ratio and association. And ratio is a type of association which is rendered quantitative. Thus it can be seen that association underlies all the operations of the material mind.

41. Quantitative and Evaluative Thinking

Where logical implication alone is concerned, mathematics and verbal reasoning are quantitative forms of thinking. For both mathematical and verbal concepts are related as units. Thus the equation $2 + 3 = 5$, stating an implication of equality, asserts that two addends compose a sum.

The addends are quantified terms of the equation in the sense that they are units themselves (the number 2 and the number 3), not in the sense that they are pluralities of arithmetical units. So to perform the operation it is not immediately necessary to know the value of the numbers. They can yield to a temporary substitution by symbols, as in $x + y = z$. This is what makes algebraic expression possible.

Likewise, the verbal proposition, "all dogs are mammals," relates dogs to mammals in the same way. It can be "all p are q" (or "if p then q"). Dogs and mammals are quantified terms of the proposition in which they occur. They are units of relation. Consequently, they can be anything. For their content is a matter of indifference.

It is only in an independent reference to their signification that they must be recognized for what they are. So, given this purely structural role, it would be permissible to transfer these terms from proposition to proposition without an immediate concern for their meanings, if new terms were not being continually introduced.

However, associative thinking does occur prior to the placement of terms within a set of statements. It could not be otherwise. For one of three forms of associative thinking must take place if a relationship between the terms is to be recognized. Either like properties are related, unlike properties are contrasted, or, as mentioned previously, a relationship is assumed without a specific reference to the properties of the subject term. Thus, in the latter case, the statement "all (or some) houses are liquid" joins the units houses and liquid in an unlikely relationship of properties: liquid houses.

So it is in these three ways that the imaginative process of associative comparison relates two concepts prior to their becoming the subject and predicate of a proposition: They have properties in common. They do not have the properties under consideration in common. Or they are assumed to have certain properties in common, though it is not evident. All propositions in a subsequent chain of verbal reason follow

The Thinking Process

this pattern of relations, though they are derivative (as in the conclusion of a syllogism).

An associative comparison takes place prior to the formation of initial or new statements. For it is made when concepts are regarded in the manner of images. In other words, it occurs when concepts are treated as yet unformed—as imagery—so that a comparison of individual properties may take place.

But, once the statements are formed, the associated concepts are committed to a process of logical manipulation. Logical transitions take place in light of the comparisons already made. For the relations between terms have been recognized by means of their supporting images (their properties). And it is this reasoning process alone, as opposed to the associative process, which is referred to as quantitative thinking. The associative process is evaluative thinking, due to its preoccupation with an alignment (or nonalignment) of properties.

Say the human mind had at a previous time abstracted the concept "dog" from an investigation of many dogs of different character. The characteristics of these dogs would have been made present to imagination in the form of images. The mind would have identified those properties which dogs have in common. In this way, it would have defined the concept "dog." In other words, having abstracted certain properties and placed them in the classification "dog," it quantified them as a verbal unit.

Now associative thinking, in developing yet another concept, may have observed that cats, dogs, horses, etc. all nurse their young. So it isolated the property "lactation," along with several other properties, and grouped the animals possessing them into the classification "mammals." Thus a new classification was made. And the concept "mammals" also became a quantifiable unit.

So, in a later act of thinking, the mind recalls the concepts "dogs" and "mammals" from memory, remembering how they are related. It notes that many of the essential properties of the classification "dogs" are included among the properties of "mammals." Thus it is enabled to form a proposition which predicates mammals of dogs. The two concepts, "dogs" and "mammals," are thus associated in a statement as logical terms. They are placed together in "all dogs are mammals."

Now, in proceeding with the logical manipulation of subjects and predicates between statements, there is an oversight which occurs. For reasoning omits an acknowledgement of evaluative thinking. But evaluative thinking is not only important. It is markedly different from quantitative thinking. For it is distinguished by the fact that it weighs its considerations.

It relates things on a scale of human preference. For example, if a person at a horse race were to make the judgment, "this is the fastest horse," she would not be making a technical distinction between individuals of the species. She would be evaluating the horse in terms of her betting interest.

In matters of a deeper significance, evaluative thinking in general does something similar. It leads to judgments of a greater significance, as in the attribution of the concepts "beauty" and "wisdom." Examples of judgments employing these concepts would be, "this is a beautiful sunset" or "that is a wise person."

The Thinking Process

"Beauty" arises between a person and something she considers beautiful. It is a relationship. And it is subjective in character. Again, the concept "wisdom" expresses a person's evaluation of another person concerning the latter person's breadth of understanding. Thus the attribution of both "beauty" and "wisdom" involves personal judgment.

Accordingly, each statement is subjective, though it may be supposed to incorporate the view of others. It suggests a hierarchy of importance. Likewise, in what appears to be a less personal case, such as an association of mammals with dogs, a person also establishes a hierarchy of preference. For there is an evaluation. It is that dogs *should* be included among mammals.

So, in the statement "all houses are liquid" a person is affirming what must to her be the case. She is making an evaluative judgment. It does not matter if she does or does not have empirical evidence to back her claim. Consequently, considering the foundational importance and breadth of its range, evaluative thinking should not be ignored. For doing so omits consideration of the subjective element in objective relations.

42. Foundational Concepts

The four foundational concepts in Aristotelian logic are existence, nonexistence, greater, and less.[32] The first two of

---

[32] Aristotle, *Logic*.

these concepts are expressed by the copulas, "is" and "is not." The subject of a statement either is or is not possessed of a specific predicate property. In other words, the attribution exists, or it does not exist, within the conditions of the statement. The third and fourth foundational concepts apply to the quantifiers, "all" and "some," "all" being greater than "some," and "some" being less than "all."

Aristotelian logic provides a framework for understanding the reasoning process. It clarifies the relationships between concepts. It also underlies conditional propositions. Consequently, the four concepts—existence, nonexistence, greater, and less—extend well beyond the confines of Aristotelian logic.

Greater and less are employed in any conceptual relation. They apply to matters of equality (neither greater nor less), and inequality, similarity, and dissimilarity, which latter are either greater or less. In other words, the properties of a predicate are attributed or denied to some portion of the subject.

If a person says, "She is tall," he is attributing tallness to a subject. He is asserting that it exists for that subject. If he says "she is not tall," he is asserting its nonexistence for the subject. So it becomes a question of the existence or nonexistence of the predicate property in the subject. But this is a matter of greater or less as well, depending upon what portion of the subject shares or does not share properties with the predicate.

Let it be assumed that two sets of properties which have nothing in common do exist, one within the subject and the other within the predicate of a statement. Such is the case concerning the proposition "She is not tall." The predicate has the property of tallness which the subject does not. No

The Thinking Process

other properties are pertinent, other than the gender and humanity of the subject, which are not under consideration in the predicate, since it only deals with tallness. So the subject and predicate are distinguished from one another by properties which they do not have in common.

This being the case, the subject and predicate are different in kind, yet are simultaneous in existence within the thought. It is in this way that a subject can partake of exclusion in relation to its predicate. It does not exhibit those properties which are predicated as not being of it. However, both sets of properties—those of gender and personhood on the one hand, and those of tallness on the other—do exist in the thought.

But they are excluded from one another. The predicate does not exist in the subject. And the subject does not exist in the predicate. Thus the conditions of existence apply in two ways: both subject and predicate exist, but not within one another. Greater or less is also seen to apply. For the subject is understood to be lacking the properties of the predicate. It is therefore less in that sense.

These circumstances concerning verbal expression having been considered, it is also worth noting that the four foundational concepts of logic, which are existence, nonexistence, greater, and less, are equivalent to the mathematical concepts: unity, zero, addition, and subtraction. The expression of any number other than zero indicates the existence of a quantity (or unity of one or more arithmetical units) within a thought, even if it takes the form of a negative integer. And zero correlates to the nonexistence of a quantity.

To make a mathematical statement is to give existence to its terms within the statement. And to form a judgment concerning a change in quantity is to affirm not only that the change exists within the mathematical thought, but to determine that it results in greater or less. For example, to deter-determine a square root is to arrive at less than the square. So the four mathematical concepts correlate to the four fundamental concepts of logic.

43. Logic and Will

The faculty of reason is not to be revealed in a mysterious and inexplicable place beyond material experience. For it is a creation of the intuitions of unity, plurality, and totality. It is these which combine to form the conceptual powers of abstraction and classification. And it is classification which makes possible the rules of logic. Classification, therefore, constitutes a basis for the formal structure of logical systems of thought.

The mind cannot organize experience, unless it recognizes a unity. It cannot extract meaning from unity, unless it recognizes a plurality within the unity or between one unit and another. And there would be no reason for it to perform either of these operations, if the unfolding process of reason did not pursue a totality of interrelations in its elaboration of meaning.

The formal structure of logic develops extended relationships between classifications. The totality of these classifications, when placed in logical relations, is linked together in a system which exhibits a sense of inevitability,

The Thinking Process

generally referred to as logical necessity. This is impressive. However, upon close examination, it can be seen that logical necessity is an expression of the force of human will.

The will is embedded in consciousness. And consciousness is an elemental unity which lies at the foundation of material experience. For it underlies the mental impressions which are the substance of that experience. And it initiates the intuitions which structure it. Thus it is the organizational source of experience, both in the order of its presentation of mental impressions to the mind and in its articulation of them for the understanding, where it impresses its unity upon them in various ways.

In accordance with the first intuition, the mind seeks unity in an object of mental apprehension, so that it may be experienced intelligibly. It seeks further unity in the progression of thought. Hence the desire for unity results in a strong inclination toward a systematic development of logical relationships. Once formed, the logical relationships are felt to be necessary. For they are in accordance with the ever-present will to impose unity.

This is particularly evident in an analytic proposition like "all fathers are men with children," with its seemingly irrefutable certainty. But the irrefutability of such a statement is derived from the matching properties of its terms. In other words, the impulse behind logical necessity in this case is based on a drive for unity, resulting in a recognition of identity between the terms of the proposition.

It is in this manner that the properties of logical terms are related, even when they are not analytic. For, in a statement such as "some men are tall," there is an assumption of identity between the properties of "some men" and "tall."

However, the identity is not explicit prior to the predication of "tall" to "some men." Therefore, it is not irrefutable.

So it can be understood that consciousness is the ground of human experience. And the will is expressed within it. As a consequence, in assimilating material experience to understanding, the will seeks to bring it into an integrated unity. In other words, it strives to create the simple unity from which it originates. Beginning with this, the will's inclination is bolstered by the practical usefulness of the systematic relations of concepts developed in logical thought. Thus the mind succumbs to the will's impulse by believing such relations necessary.

44. Tentative Knowledge

If a person considers William Harvey's view of the circulatory system,[33] she will encounter a scientific explanation which presents itself with greater accuracy than any previously kindred biological view. It works well. And it has been substantiated by subsequent research. So it represents an excellent mapping of the manner in which the heart and blood appear to function together within the body. His observations and conclusions have stood the test of four centuries. Thus today they lie at the core of modern cardiovascular medicine.

---

[33] William Harvey, *An Anatomical Disquisition on The Motion of the Heart and Blood in Animals*.

The Thinking Process

So one can hardly imagine an argument which would refute them.

But none of the evidence makes the theory true. For a theory is a map. It is not the thing mapped. It subsists within a structure of thought and investigative procedure which are peculiar to the culture in which they are formed. And, though all the world should adopt it, it is but a particular view. Since maps can take alternate forms, this one might have been different, in spite of the evidence a close analysis provides.

Had the general environment of thought and procedure been otherwise in Harvey's age, the theory might have been worked out in an alternative way, in spite of the close uniformity between thought and observation in the practical results of its physical investigations. For the overarching structure of thought would have been different.

To better understand this, it is useful to imagine a situation in which the Chinese should have had no contact with the West. They would have continued to advance their culture in isolation from the West. And, as their science grew, an alternative way of understanding the internal workings of the body might have been developed to a degree as practically successful as Harvey's. Perhaps more so. Perhaps in some ways that is the case now.

This alternative understanding could have been as effective as Harvey's in explaining whatever phenomena were observed and their practical results. And the fact that this could be the case, and has been to a greater or less extent, demonstrates the tentative character of human knowledge. For knowledge is in varying degrees culturally dependent.

Consequently, it can be seen that, in spite of an inalterable uniformity of observational detail, Harvey's explanation is the outcome of a specific environment of thought. For his explanation could have been otherwise in its conceptual organization. Nevertheless, it must be conceded that his system does present a formidable case.

Its replacement by an alternative theory is hardly imaginable. For, should that have been the case, it would have required a complete restructuring of mental precedents—a different world view. But such an alternative structuring is at least possible. It is possible not only for Harvey, but for the entire scientific world view.

45. Plato's Eternal Ideas

Eternal ideas were central to Plato's thinking. For he held that material objects were imperfect exemplars of them.[34] These ideas were lodged both in the mind of man and in the eternal mind of God. Objects encountered in material experience were understood to be inexact expressions of eternal concepts because the objects were continually coming into and going out of being. In other words, the objects shifted into and out of definitional form. This gave them intellectual instability.

Perhaps, if human awareness were more inclusive of change, human beings could recognize as one the various disparate but related manifestations of an object. A green apple, a ripe apple, an overripe apple, a spoiled apple are ap-

---

[34] Plato, *The Republic.*

The Thinking Process

ples. And the many may be recognized as a complete expression of one.

But such a recognition will not come without a close examination over time, resulting in a reflection upon the development of the various phases of the object. Nevertheless, there is something essential about objects which distinguishes them from one another regardless of development. It is this which groups them into classifications. For human beings can recognize a community of properties belonging to one object. In Plato's view, that community of properties is the eternal idea, which is apprehended by the mind alone.

For example, take a chair. In physical experience, many different kinds of chairs are found: blue ones, red ones, high ones, low ones, chairs under construction, fully completed chairs, and those which are in a state of dilapidation or disintegration. So what is to be made of them? A chair is what? If one variation is selected for emphasis, the chosen sample will represent some but not all chairs. So what is it that makes it specifically a chair?

To understand this, a person must enquire into its essence, its universal characteristics. And these are the properties which are its definition. If successful, a definition succinctly and unmistakably describes what endures throughout all variations. As a result, a person can be assured as to when he encounters a chair and when he encounters a closely similar but different object, such as a three-legged stool.

But there is an important limiting feature to any definition. It can only describe something by relating it to something else. Without context there is nothing. So the definition of a chair is that it is an object made by a human craftsperson for the purpose of a person being able to sit comfortably upon it. This definition holds even if the craftsperson operates equipment which makes a plastic chair. The essential definition has been stated elsewhere. But for the purpose of illustrating the concept, it is further elaborated here.

As it appears, such a definition might include benches and three-legged milking stools. But benches lack the suggestion of personal use. And three-legged stools are usually low and unstable. They are both quite similar to a chair and fulfill some of its purpose. But they lack the precision of purpose attributed to a chair. For one assumes that a chair should be reasonably personal and comfortable. So benches and milking stools are not chairs.

Now a bucket may be turned over and put to use as a chair. But one would be inclined to say that it is being used *as* a chair, not that it *is* a chair. This is because the bucket, though made by a human craftsperson, was not made for the purpose of being sat upon. Thus the essential definition of a chair does not apply to buckets.

Nor would a large, smooth boulder fall under the definition of a chair because, though a person might comfortably sit upon the boulder, it is not a product of human craftsmanship. So the bucket fails in purpose and the boulder in origin. They are therefore not chairs. They are substitutes for chairs.

It is easy to see that origin relates the chair to its source. It has an origin in human manufacture. This is a relationship to something else. And the chair's purpose is again relational. For it relates to those who will be making use of it. In this, as in its origin, nothing of the chair's material or shape is mentioned.

The Thinking Process

These factors are significant only insofar as they contribute to the chair's origin and purpose. A craftsperson is constrained in the use of materials and design only by the chair's origin and purpose. He will likely not make one of emerald because he cannot afford to. And he will not use paper in its construction because it will not bear the weight of a person.

So, if something is defined in terms of its relationship to other things, it is being classified in this way. And, though a classification can be expressed in terms of physical properties alone, like a chemical or physical definition of a substance, such an expression would not constitute a full and final classification. For to be classified, its properties must exhibit both an origin and a human relation.

For example, benzene is a toxic, flammable hydrocarbon obtained from coal tar and used in making dyes and synthetic rubber. And quicksand is a mixture of water and rounded grains of sand which tends to engulf whatever lies on its surface. How these things came about and their relationship to human beings, both positive and negative, is essential to a full expression of what they are.

So a chair might be described as a wooden, metal, or plastic object with a back, a horizontal surface, and four legs. But this makes clear the difficulty of a purely descriptive classification. For physical properties provide a far less determinate understanding of an object than origin and purpose. Hence the greater utility of the latter elements in forming a classification.

To elaborate, let a random assortment of chemical elements or a disparate collection of geometrical figures be imagined. The former of these exhibits individually unique physical and chemical properties and the latter specific delineations of figure. But their useful interrelations were only partially understood until the former were arranged in a periodic table by Mendeleev and the latter in Euclid's logically organized system. It is in terms of these purpose-oriented classifications, which contribute to an understanding of origin as well, that human beings now think of them. For, as the classifications come to reveal origin and purpose, they more closely relate their topic to human interest.

But regardless of the type of classification, partial or full, descriptive or purposeful, any relationship between classifications can be represented by encompassing, overlapping, or separate Euler circles, depending upon the manner of the sharing of properties. For example, chairs can be understood as a type of furniture. In this way, they are subsumed within a more comprehensive classification: furniture.

Whereas stools are understood as exhibiting some but not all the properties of a chair. In the former instance, furniture has an expanded relation to a chair. It includes other things with it. And, in the latter instance, stools have a restricted relation to a chair. The restricted relationship is represented by overlapping circles. For chairs and stools are classifications which share kindred properties, but not other properties.

Not only chairs and stools, but chairs and beds are of this relationship. All three are made by human craftsmen for human use. And they may be composed of similar materials, though they do not share an identical physical form. So they do not serve identical purposes. People sit on chairs. But they use stools for a narrower purpose, which includes sit-

The Thinking Process

ting, but in a rather unsatisfactory manner. And they lie on beds. That is what those items are designed for.

Beyond these examples, there are classifications which appear to have little or nothing in common. In fact, so great is their divergence that, even where there is some point of commonality between them, they are, for convenience sake, generally classed as having nothing in common. So let an extreme illustration of this be entertained. Rainwater and fire will serve the purpose. And let the association between them be limited to a description without mention of origin or purpose.

The descriptive character alone of a physical phenomenon is immediately apparent to human awareness. For it permits observation without reflection forming an associative connection in the mind. By this standard, rainwater and fire appear to have nothing in common. But, in fact, they must have something in common. For the act of relating things—i.e., of bringing them into the same context—implies a connection between them.

Thus, since all extant things are related as existing in one universe, it may be assumed that there must always be a way of establishing an associative relationship between two things. Accordingly, it can be asserted that both rainwater and fire express physical being. Each physical object comes into being, expresses being, and passes out of it.[35]

In addition, each object exists in relationship to all other physical entities existing in the past, present, or future. For example, there are causal relations. Thus this would include

---

[35] Fire, though conceived as an expression of energy, is an object of human awareness. Consequently, it is also physical.

an object's relationship to physical entities which either have not yet come into physical being, when it is itself extant, or those which have already passed out of physical being.

So things similar to rainwater and those akin to fire (vapor in the first instance and heat in the second) would express gradations of association in that relation—i.e. varying similarities and differences. In other words, vapor would be somewhat different from rainwater. And heat alone would be somewhat different from fire. Thus, in traversing the realm of physical entities, gradual reductions of likeness from either rainwater or fire can be traced.

Accordingly, gradations of similitude would incrementally decrease until rainwater and fire approached a point where they would become more different but would also meet in mutual likeness. That point would be dissimilar to both rainwater and fire. But it would also be similar to them. The intermediate point could be any number of things at any distance from the sources.

It would depend upon the chain of relations which was followed in divergence from the sources. One thing it could lead to is steam. That would be an intermediate point which would connect rainwater with fire. For steam is water, though not rainwater. And it is heat, which is not fire, but a physical property of fire.

In this example, a definition including origin and purpose has been avoided. And descriptive relationships between physical properties have been emphasized. For a reference to origin and purpose was not desired. If they were, they would constitute a full and final definition. Yet, when the usefulness of rainwater or fire is considered, not to mention the inconveniences in some instances, these properties come

The Thinking Process

readily to mind. And they are reiterated in the character of steam. For steam is useful. And it can burn.

Anything whatsoever is either directly or indirectly useful, even if a knowledge of its harmfulness or obstructing uselessness is what is useful. This is so, regardless of whether or not its usefulness is emphasized in a description. Otherwise, human beings would have no interest in the thing and would discard it from consideration. But even so, everything eventually gets classified according to human interest.

Thus everything has, potentially or explicitly, a full and final definition which is not limited to a description of its physical properties. The definition is based on its relationship to human interest. And what all definitions and their interrelationships demonstrate is that they are necessary to human understanding.

Let it be assumed that a person should encounter the properties, "cold," "round," and "white." He would recognize by their proximate association in space and time that they are a snowball. A snowball also occurs under such-and-such weather conditions. And it is made by human hands. So the human origin of the snowball is acknowledged. Furthermore, it is noted that it has numerous purposes, from engaging in a snow fight to making a snowman. Since the snowball does not occur naturally, it exhibits the express purpose of being made available to be thrown or made into something.

Thus there is an origin and a purpose. The snowball's definition is enclosed within a concept. So thinking about the snowball and its properties leads to an assessment of its use. In this way, the mind classifies it according to a human interest, which means it undergoes an evaluation: What is it good for? How important is that?

Now, if a concept embraces a universal definition, it is a universal classification, since all concepts are classifications, whether they be universal or particular. So a concept may reference something particular, such as "Socrates." Or it may reference a plurality, such as "the two philosophers, Socrates and Plato."

But it may also reference something universal, such as "philosophers." In this case, it references the properties, rather than the thing. In other words, it focuses upon the definition. For the singular class "Socrates" contains one individual. The plural class "two philosophers" contains two individuals. But the universal class "philosophers" contains no specific individuals.

Any concept—particular, plural, or universal—can be associated with any other concept through a string of relationships between them. There are separate strings of associations concerning any set of concepts. Thus, for example, the term "Socrates" exhibits multiple strings of relationships to other concepts.

A string of relationships is a family of properties among multiple concepts, including all the middle concepts between the two being related, in which no one property is shared by them all. So "Socrates" can be related to "a robin's nest" by such an intermediate progression of concepts as "man," "animal," "bird," and "nest."

Again, putting aside the property "rational thinker," an association with Socrates may be made on the basis of his being a man of intellectual insight. He may then be compared to Emerson the sage and to a writer of the Indian

The Thinking Process

Upanishads, as well. On the other hand, by means of a different association, he may be compared to Euripides and Shakespeare. For, like Socrates, they are men of creative intellect.

These are only the starting points. Strings of association extend indefinitely. Moreover, it is clear that terms at any level of abstraction can be associated with terms at every other level: universal with plural, plural with singular, singular with universal. All concepts have their complement anywhere in the community of concepts.

Either directly or indirectly, concepts originate from experience. The properties of the objects they define have a physical character, which is to say the concepts reference physical properties. And they are given a human origin in the discovery of their purpose. For the purpose assigns to them a human significance. Thus, even when they are not made by human agency, the recognition of their significance provides them with a human origin. For the discovery of their significance initiates their entrance into the human family of fully recognizable and useful concepts.

Once the defining concepts are formed, there are flexible relations among them. They can undergo not only processes of association, but processes of dissociation. In fact, a recognition of similarities must be accompanied by a recognition of dissimilarities. For without dissimilarities, concepts could not be isolated one from another. Socrates the philosopher is like the sage Emerson. But he is also unlike him. He is even more like the philosopher Plato. But so is he unlike him.

In addition to their flexible associations, concepts may be reworked in the imagination, altering them from one set of images representing specific properties to another set of images representing altered properties. The new set of images would then form a new concept which is distinct from the first. Yet it would have a discernible relationship to it. This is easily seen if the two concepts only differ in a few properties. But, even if all the properties were changed one after another, a relationship would remain. Otherwise, the alteration could not have occurred.

Given all these circumstances, it can be readily understood why Aristotle rejected the independent existence of eternal ideas.[36] For, were it the case that eternal ideas existed in the manner developed by Plato, there would be an indeterminate array of them in infinite gradations of signification. And none of them could be created, but only discovered, by the human mind.

In addition, any imperfect knowledge derived from the ever-changing forms of nature would, according to the conception of the eternal ideas, present the human mind with an unreliable instrument of thought. Its concepts would be vague and uncertain, not like those of the eternal ideas. So such an approach to human reason would not only trivialize experience. It would have rendered scientific study unlikely. For this reason, Aristotle held that the mind simply abstracts its concepts from experience.

For example, the definition of a chair, according to Aristotle, is not separate from an existing chair. It is inherent in it. It is therefore not an eternal idea. For it comes to exist in a mind as a thought derived from experience. But the problem with Aristotle's view is that questions remain: How does ab-

---

[36] Aristotle, *Metaphysics*.

The Thinking Process

straction come about?[37] How does the recognition of a physical object or the formation of a thought about it occur? These questions must be answered by a direct observation of the workings of the mind.

An awareness of the unity of the properties in an object cannot have originated with the object. For each property also constitutes a unity. There is at the least a unity of mental impressions, or qualities, within each property. Thus either to perceive or to classify is to gather mental impressions or properties into a unity. But there is no material explanation for the gathering process.

Unity exists in its simplest form in human consciousness. For it is a characteristic of consciousness alone. Having apprehended its own unity in consciousness, the mind applies it to experience in the form of a unifying focus. Accordingly, the focus functions as an intuition and is enabled to recognize associations of mental impressions as qualities of properties and the properties as informing physical objects and objects of thought.

So what is consciousness? Consciousness is immediate. It is the ground of experience. It is not a mental impression, much less a grouping of these. It is that within which they occur. It expresses no extension, no divisibility within itself. For extension and divisibility set forth the finite in material experience. They are the content of consciousness. Whereas consciousness is not finite.

---

[37] A restricted representationalist perspective is employed here, not the more inclusive immaterialist view. If the immaterialist viewpoint were to be considered, physical objects would appear in the mind. For they *are* human thoughts. Thus one would not be understood to generate the other.

Yet consciousness is as much a part of experience as any mental impression, though it is not finite. Because consciousness exhibits no material properties, the mind knows it to be *not* finite, or *in*-finite. This infinite, immutable character is seen to be eternal because it is inalterable. Thus consciousness is the eternal.

It is inalterable because, if not, it would involve a distinction and interchange among mental impressions. Change involves time, which, due to its involvement in the finite elements of motion (which motion is its measure), must be judged to be material and therefore not a characteristic of the immaterial and eternal.

So this much of Plato's eternal ideas remains: a human being is able to experience the material and to think about it because there is something immaterial and eternal in his experience and thought. But that something is not an idea. It is consciousness, which unifies the elements of experience and thought.

46. The Platonic Ideal

A discussion concerning the origin of the perfect circle might illustrate the appeal of the eternal ideas to Plato. Let it be supposed that a person is attempting to create a wheel. It would not be long before she discovers that the more uniform the curvature of its circumference, the more efficient it is likely to be. It would also become apparent that the curvature of the circumference must be rendered in reference to

The Thinking Process

the axle at the center of the wheel. For the curvature must be uniform in terms of its distance from this axle.

It is no large step for the imagination to construct a wheel with a hub, rim, and spokes (though historically it may have taken some time). The use of spokes would lighten the wheel. And the identical, or near identical, length of each spoke would provide a more or less consistent measure of the distance between the hub and the rim.

Now let the hub be designated as the center of a circle, and the rim as its circumference. The spokes represent the radius. At this point, the radius, unlike the spokes, will be of a single measure. The result will resemble Euclid's definition of a circle. However, in practice it is impossible to construct a wheel whose rim is a perfect circle. Or, if it is done, it is impossible to know it for certain. There could be a margin of error, however indistinguishable.

This is because the circumference must be subdivided into an indeterminate number of arcs to form a perfect curvature. For the distance of each arc from the hub must be established ever more minutely in terms of the size of the arcs. So, given the indeterminacy of the number of arcs, such a wheel could not be built.

Here is a concept of a perfect wheel in comparison to which all physical wheels are but imperfect facsimiles. But the concept exists only in the mind. However, it is more consistent in character than any existing physical copies. So it would seem that the idea (or form) of the perfect wheel, being inalterable by any material force, must therefore be eternal.

But the problem is that the ideal concept is an abstraction. It does not physically exist, as do the manifold wheels to be found in nature. It exists only as a concept precisely because it borrows something from all the natural examples: an attempt at a uniform curvature. And it leaves out what differentiates the natural examples: any variations in curvature. But in doing this, it leaves out what is unique to each of them, what gives each of them its individual character.

So, to insist upon the superiority of the concept over the thing would be like saying that there is one ideal human being, whereas all existing individual people are flawed with their peculiar psychological and moral characteristics. Notions such as this have saddled the world with an intolerance that persists to this day.

There is no doubt that the human mind is a powerful instrument. And there is no denying its originality, its ability to grasp essential properties while omitting the nonessential. But it must not be forgotten that the material the human mind works with, and to which it is limited, is its content of mental impressions. The majority of these are ascribed to images which represent physical experience. But the concept of a perfect wheel or circle is a creation of imagination. It arises from an ability to abstract and classify. Beyond this it has no purpose.

47. Human Experience

The scientific use of efficient-cause reasoning, combined with a general reverence for the infallibility of logic, has led to intellectual arrogance. For the success of these activities

The Thinking Process

has convinced human beings of their specialness and separateness from nature. This in turn has fostered an exploitive and destructive attitude toward nature.

But it is to be hoped that a better understanding of these mental faculties—of the character of their origin—may restore humanity to a less hubristic attitude and a more holistic approach to nature. For it is a superficial, but powerfully effective, knowledge of the material world which has led to this problem.

The awareness of a world ordered in space and time supplies the content of physical experience. Insofar as thought alone is taken into consideration, mental representations are included in this experience. For they are conditioned according to the ordering of space and time. So let it be asserted that all of sensory and much of mental activity comprise material experience.

Now, because thoughts are not the whole of mental activity, a problem emerges. It is that the mental representations of material phenomena do not reflect every aspect of experience. Consequently, that experience must include something other than the material. So, to be inclusive of the fullness of experience, human awareness must be understood in a broader sense than is entertained by a scientific worldview. For this view limits verification of its hypotheses to the data of the senses, which is the reason the operations of the mind are generally interpreted in sensory terms.

It is true that Locke[38] acknowledges the operations of the mind as playing a separate role from the senses. But he does

---

[38] John Locke, *An Essay Concerning Human Understanding*.

not make a ground for them clear. Hume[39] also speaks of relations of ideas as opposed to matters of fact. But again, it is matters of fact which dominate the discussion. Relations of ideas simply exist without explanation of their origin.

On the other hand, Berkeley[40] does not make a distinction between mental operations and physical phenomena. For all are enclosed within the mind: *esse est percipi* (to be is to be perceived). So, among these three thinkers, the problem of establishing a ground for the operations of the mind is not resolved.

It is not until Kant[41] that an understanding of the mind's more comprehensive character is brought into focus. For in his view it is the mind itself, together with the intuitions of space, time, and sensation, which creates human experience. The mind exhibits a direct instrumentality in forming a basis upon which knowledge is constructed.

But what he fails to do is uncover the foundation which lies beyond the faculty of reason. For he does not extend his insight beyond the categories. So the present investigation must be taken a step further: reason should be accounted for in terms of something more fundamental than the categories.

In light of these considerations, it will be acknowledged, as has previously been the case,[42] that material experience is a construct of the human mind. It is composed of mental impressions arranged by the mind into spatial and temporal

---

[39] David Hume, *A Treatise of Human Nature and An Enquiry Concerning Human Understanding*.
[40] George Berkeley, *The Principles of Human Knowledge and Three Dialogues between Hylas and Philonous*.
[41] Immanuel Kant, *The Critique of Pure Reason*.
[42] George Tollefson, *The Immaterial Structure of Human Experience*.

The Thinking Process

extensions. The extensions are physical objects and objects of thought. Their qualities are the mental impressions. But extension itself is not a quality. Rather, it is the means by which the mind integrates unity with plurality in terms of contiguity, simultaneity, and sequence. Out of this comes an awareness of both physical and mental space.

Beyond the original formation of the extensions of physical and mental space, which are expressed in the mind by means of imagery, experience continues to develop. New mental impressions are formed into imagery. And concepts are created from past and present images. Logical structures then arise to supply the concepts with relations and reason with operating principles. For it is by this means that concepts are linked together in ever more sophisticated constructions.

So, in accordance with the maturing activity of the mind, experience becomes increasingly an expression of reason. It is overlaid with a conceptual veneer which facilitates an intellectual understanding of its varied relations. However, this is by no means a shallow overlay. For it penetrates and intermingles with the original foundation.

Thus determining what is foundation and what is overlay can become problematic. It is for this reason that few adults revisit their infantile impressions. Hence the loss of innocence and wonder born of free association, which was a feature of childhood and is no longer recognized in adult sensibility.

Once a foundation of experience is laid down by means of imagery in early childhood, it is subsequently made conceptually available to the maturing mind. The conceptual apprehension evolves. And, as it is divided by the intellect into physical and mental spheres, the mind begins to increasingly understand the physical as separate from itself. Moreover, as both mental and physical events are presented in sequence, there are clearly demarked segments of time. Instead of simultaneity, prior and subsequent are recognized. Thus, as one thing precedes another, thoughts become reactions to other thoughts.

Again, thoughts begin as direct representations of experience. But some of these early images are modified imaginatively. And concepts are fashioned from both kinds of images: the direct representations and the modified imagery. Derivative concepts—concepts made from other concepts—then appear by means of a modification of the internal imagery of prior concepts, thus producing varying levels of abstraction.

Temporally associated series of images represent events. And these may also be converted to concepts, which can be raised to varying levels of abstraction. As experience progresses, concepts of events are brought together in causal relations. By such means, experience is rendered increasingly articulate. That is to say, it is translated into an intellectual overlay. The overlay incorporates logical structures, which include idealized languages like mathematics.

In consideration of this transition from image to concept to systematic thought, it can be said that any role the mind plays in evolving the structure of experience must begin with isolated representations, or images. For it is these which are converted into concepts. Consequently, reason, which employs concepts, can be understood as disciplined imagination.

The Thinking Process

However, given this process, reason should not be misunderstood as a final and sole operative in the formation of mature experience. For the initial foundation is enriched, not eliminated, by the overlay. Consciousness continues to play its ground role, not only in supplying mental impressions, but in determining their order of presentation. Thus it continues to control the initial formation of imagery prior to its imaginative modification and its conceptual transformation.

The order of presentation arises from the sequence of mental impressions. As they appear, they are associatively grouped into the extensions of physical objects and objects of thought. Accordingly, since events involve objects, the order of presentation determines the order in which events take place. Thus the order of events is not determined by the will of the person who is aware of it.

Consciousness is not to be conceived as material experience. For it plays only a formative role through the intuitions of unity, plurality, and totality. The intuitions form the extensions of objects of thought from the sequences of mental impressions. And it is these objects of thought which construct material experience.

The mind is not aware of the origin of mental impressions. They simply appear to it. Consciousness is their source. It does not know how. It is simply aware that it is. But it does not apprehend itself as a mere background for experience either. For it appears before itself as an unconstructed unity and participates in experience.

The recognition of this unconstructed unity arises from the fact that consciousness is experienced as indivisible and without discernible bounds. Yet it has a content which is divisible and limited. The content is initially encountered as an unknown something. Hence it is differentiated from its medium as that unknown something. The medium encompasses it and functions as an occasion for its unification.

Thus an intuition of unity is established. This is the mind's faculty of attention, or focus, concerning the whole or some portion of its content. By means of this faculty, the mind is enabled to vary its content. It can move from a full content to a lesser portion, or vice versa. Thus a new sphere of content is a portion or an enlarged encompassment of the previous.

Now the mind cannot simultaneously entertain a clear focus on more than a single mental impression. Yet it is a comparison of two which establishes the articulation of any impression as finite. So this demands a sequence of thoughts. But the mind receives such a sequence so rapidly, that it appears as though it has been received at once.

Moreover, a sequence of some particular length may also be repeated, creating a sense of duration and a conviction that the whole is unified. This is an association of impressions. When an association of mental impressions is fixed in awareness so that it may be recognized in future situations, it becomes an extension of thought, which is an image. And a plurality of such associations must occur and be repeated to create and sustain a field of focus.

So an increasing articulation of awareness is made possible. And by the same means, a plurality of extensions is established so that subsequently it may be built upon by imagination and intellect. It is in this way that mental objects assume a temporal sequence and the physical objects some of them represent are brought together in spatial contiguity and temporal sequence. Accordingly, material experience

The Thinking Process

arises as a domain of objects of thought and of physical objects.

So consciousness is the cause of the expression of unity in the mind. Thus it provides for an awareness of various limited manifestations of unity. So, besides a general awareness, the gift of consciousness to the mind is this sense of unity. It renders material experience possible by giving it the means of becoming an articulated and integrated structure.

When active consciousness is spoken of, it is as a source of the intuition of unity. Thus a reference is being made to its separate content. For it is upon this that unification is performed. Therefore, the unifier and that which is unified are distinct from one another. The unifier is consciousness. The unified is its content.

But, once the intuition of unity has been exercised, any further reference to an active consciousness is discarded from consideration. The intuition is applied in varying patterns of focus, thereby establishing a multitude of differentiated finite unities. It is in this way that an active consciousness becomes the intuition of unity. It is present as a faculty of discernment. Consequently, the recognition of unities is prior to every kind of subsequent articulation.

However, this intuition does not stand alone. There are additional intuitions: those of plurality and totality. The intuition of plurality is necessitated by the fact that the first intuition's encounter with mental impressions only differentiates between unities which appear sequentially in the mind.

They must be rendered individually distinct from one another as qualities and feelings. And this depends upon a recognition of the unique effect which each distinct impression makes upon the mind. Only subsequent to these first two intuitions does the intuition of totality arise, when the intuition of unity is reapplied to some portion of such a recognized plurality.

As far as human awareness is concerned, all three intuitions are immediate. For, as fundamental instruments of discernment, they are unknown to human awareness. It is their effects which are known. Thus the three intuitions precede the general ordering of experience. Consequently, they are prior to any development of thought content or representation of physical phenomena.

Now, because it is an expression of universal consciousness, the origin of the mental impressions is also unaccounted for in human awareness. So is the general sequential character of their appearance. But it does not follow that this order of appearance is identical to the order of phenomena. This is due to the physical, and thus temporal, complexity in the mental development of physical space. For this must take into account not only sequential relations, but simultaneous as well. Thus the initial ordering of mental impressions differs from the temporal ordering of events.

Nevertheless, the former supplies content to the latter. So it follows that the original order of mental impressions underlies and largely regulates the order of events, given a certain latitude in the structuring of spatial contiguity and its effect upon perception. But, other than feelings, only events, both mental and physical, are recognizable to a maturing human awareness. For, except when focusing upon feelings and distinct qualities, the mind does not dwell on individual mental impressions.

So contiguity of appearance has been added to sequence in temporal arrangements. And, since the recognition of time

The Thinking Process

is based upon changes among and within the extensions of physical experience, the contiguity of these extensions does indeed affect the order of events. Not everything is sequenced there as it is among the mental impressions as initially encountered. For some of those mental impressions are maintained in a simultaneous spatial order.

Thus the flow of mental impressions is instrumental, but not identical, to the orderly presentation of material events. For it is the order of this flow which determines material experience, albeit that the arranging of the mental impressions according to spatial relations also plays a role.

Thought is the chief instrument of material awareness. It is by means of the recognition of unity that the mind creates thought. This includes representations of physical experience, imaginative inventions taken loosely from the qualities and properties of these representations, and conceptualizations. In a maturing mind, conceptual thought contributes increasingly to an understanding of experience. In doing so, it contributes to its structure.

The intuitions also articulate finitude for the mind. Thus a recognition of unity, of a limitation of that unity by other unities, and of multiple unities brought together as one unity are the specific means by which human awareness recognizes finitude. These finite unities apply to individual mental impressions, extensions of thought, and extensions of physical objects. Consequently, without the intuition of unity, which is derived from the immediate experience of consciousness, imaginative representation and rational thought could not occur.

The intuition of plurality is derived from an encounter with the mental impressions. When confronted with the distinction which occurs between individual impressions—say yellow and blue—the sense of unity without articulated bounds becomes a sense of limited unity with articulated bounds. For these bounds apply to each mental impression as it is entertained in the mind in proximity to another.

Different impressions cannot be apprehended simultaneously because the mind is limited to the exercise of focus. So the intuition of plurality, or individual limitation, arises. Thus each mental impression, as an independent unity, limits the other. Their recognition as occurring in a sequence also establishes the rudiments of time, which is altered in duration, but not direction, by the contiguous arrangements of space.

From the intuition of unity together with the intuition of plurality the intuition of totality is formed. For there may be a unity, or totality, of individually limited things. For example, one can distinguish that there is a total of five apples in one bowl and a total of three in another. And there is another total of eight altogether. Or, limiting the example to qualities, there is a preponderance (or greater totality) of yellow in one object and blue in another. These qualities are feelings which, when they are combined with other qualities in an object, are not generally apprehended as independent.

So, from the three intuitions, founded originally upon a delineation of mental impressions, the human mind derives its capacity to unify, subdivide, and classify. It carries this over into the structuring of the extensions which make up the objects of thought and physical experience. And from these it recognizes a world.

Phenomena can be recognized and associated in classifications. And this inaugurates an iterative process. For, once

The Thinking Process

several classifications are determined, they may be classified together in turn. More limited classifications are encompassed partially or totally by more inclusive ones, thus bring-bringing about a relationship between them. This process is deductive reason.

It is the three intuitions working together which provide human awareness with a means for associating mental impressions as qualities in one property and for associating multiple properties in one object. Subsequently, mental classifications are formed and interrelated on the basis of properties, associating or contrasting the properties with others like or unlike them.

Thus it is by means of classifications and the properties they encompass that the properties of concepts are likened to, or differentiated from, one another in varying degrees. Such comparisons are accomplished through a recognition of similarity or dissimilarity between the properties, including those of objects of thought which are imaginatively invented or idealized and do not represent specific physical objects. Their properties nevertheless derive their origin from properties representing objects of physical experience.

It is this associative mental capacity which is the basis for the structure of logic. For logic is the cement holding deductive reasoning together. It is the interrelationship of classifications according to properties. But, because human beings are accustomed to thinking linearly, moving quickly from proposition to proposition, they often fail to notice the associations which are involved. In fact, the mind moves so rapidly that what is occurring does not appear to be associative thinking at all.

Now sometimes associations between concepts cannot be affirmed. To say "Adam is the first man" cannot be demonstrated because the "first man" property of Adam cannot be adduced. It is assumed, based on the text of a scripture. Nonetheless, whatever the means of implication, an association is made.

Any one extension, be it a thought representing a physical object or not, is limited by other extensions, each of which is a separate unity. But the limitation of one extension by another implies location. For example, this is the character of a mathematical expression. Identical quantities are separated by location in an equation, thus allowing them to perform independently of one another. Otherwise, it would not be possible to add 4 plus 4 to get 8. For one can only distinguish the one 4 from the other by its separate location in the equation, or by their prior and subsequent occurrence in thought, giving them separate temporal locations.

The situation is no different with other forms of logical thinking. Initially, all causal thinking is inductive. It begins by associating images: event q is observed to consistently follow event p. They are associated in time and place, be the events near or far from one another. And their association in this manner implies that they share the property of causation.

It is when the relationship is repeatedly observed, that the thought process settles upon its significance. It thinks: if p, then q. So the thought process begins to function deductively by converting the observed relationship into concepts. In doing so, it retains the associative character which it has carried over from repeated observation. In other words, it is observed that p and q are consistently associated by means of

The Thinking Process

time and place. A representation of this is formed in the mind, in which event p is necessarily followed by event q.

But this is to assert that p causes q. For it is to determine that p and q are fixed within a conceptual unity, which is the causal relation. And it is to assert that within this unity a property pertaining to each of the two phenomena unites them. Thus the statement, "p causes q," or "if p, then q," may be said to establish a single classification which encompasses the two classifications p and q.

It is in this manner that chemical change is understood. Chemical change is observed when an association between two chemical states is established as a result of temporal sequence and proximity of physical location. The chemical states are then further conceptually understood in terms of a quantitative transfer of elements and energy. The proportion of these quantities unites them causally. So the inclusion of elements and enhanced energy within a new compound, their release from an old one, or their transference from one to another, expresses the change.

The same sort of transference occurs in mechanical relations. A billiard ball strikes another billiard ball. And the first is observed to transfer a property of motion to the second. This too is understood according to a quantitative energy relation, which involves a displacement of energy from one ball to the other. Thus the one is said to cause the other to roll. They are causally united. The unity is a unity of change, which is conditioned by a unity of time and place. Expressed consistently, it becomes a cause-and-effect classification.

48. The Birth of Abstraction

Consciousness is infinite. But its content, which is material experience, is finite. Although a single mental impression is not spatially extended, it is the fundamental building block of the extensions, or objects, of material experience. So, if material experience is finite, mental impressions must be limited. They are limited in duration as an expression of feeling.

They are felt. Or they would not be known. Pluralities of mental impressions contribute to spatial extensions, or objects, as qualities of those extensions. Material objects are limited both spatially and in duration. Thus mental impressions are materially expressed, though individually they are not spatially extended.

So finitude implies limitation. And one of those limitations should be spatial, though a spatial property cannot be attributed to an isolated mental impression. Rather, a mental impression participates in limitation by means of its role in material experience. It either serves as a feeling, limited only in duration. Or it is a quality of an extension, the extension being limited both in space and duration.

If it were neither of these, it would be necessary to assert that it is unlimited and therefore infinite. But that which is materially finite implies absolute limitation in space and time. For to be finite is to be limited in any respect brought under consideration. Consequently, a finite entity must have parts. Otherwise, it would be indivisible, which is a characteristic of the infinite.

The Thinking Process

However, a mental impression is an apparent exception. For a mental impression exhibits no spatial extension and has no parts. Yet it varies in intensity, which is to say it can be cumulative in effect, when many instances of the same impression appear in a sequence. The intensity is a temporal matter. But its effect is as though the individual impressions were parts of a whole.

In converse distinction to finitude, *in*-finite means "not finite." It has no other meaning. It does not suggest a list of finite entities extended beyond possible computation, because, if a person could compute far enough, he would find that he had a finite number of entities acting as parts of a whole. Nor can a person divide a line into infinite points. For such points would be without the properties of limitation.

Therefore, "finite" and "infinite" are mutually exclusive concepts. Finitude indicates something which is extended and divisible, at least in a temporal sense, if not spatial. But any temporal reference implies spatial change. For time is measured in terms of spatial relations. Hence that which is only temporal can be included in material experience, since it is referenced to it. But that which is infinite, or not finite, is something which is neither extended nor divisible. Consequently, it is not material.

The unity of consciousness is the only thing which is infinite. That is why it cannot be positively defined: thinking only exhibits finite experience. Nonetheless, it is from the experience of consciousness that a person derives insight into non-limitation and indivisibility, neither of which are properties which have any concrete reference. That is why the insight can only be stated in a negative conceptual reference. The reference is to what the infinite is not.

When focused upon the realm of the finite, the unity of consciousness facilitates thought. For to think about something is to place it within focused awareness. This is focused consciousness. It is mental attention applied to the formation of a thought. In other words, to think a thought is to concentrate awareness on a specific set of mental impressions.

If they form a representation, it will be an image. But, if a definition should be applied to a set of images representing important properties, the set of images becomes an abstraction beyond that of imagery. This is because images held in support of a definition are simplified. For they play a shadow role in relation to the concept which is formed.

They can be called up in reduced representation in support of the concept. For they take on the function of ideograms which are neither wholly apparent nor absent from the mind. The purpose of these reduced images is to suggest the definition of the concept by supporting its salient properties. For the verbal definition is the concept.

By "shadow role," what is meant is that, if the concept becomes sufficiently familiar to the mind of its possessor, it can be entertained in thought with only the vaguest sense of its supporting imagery. It is in this way that, unlike a reverie of imagery, conceptual thinking can take on the characteristics of a habit.

One concept will flow logically into another in such a manner that the thought process can seem automatic. This is especially true if such a thought pattern has been rehearsed. Whereas a reverie of imagery is always fresh. Each image of it is willed at the moment of its appearance. If it is entertained in a semiconscious or unconscious mental state, it is

The Thinking Process

nevertheless followed along its meandering course with an emotional interest in its details.

Because it is a closed thought, a concept cannot be broken down. Whereas an image is an open thought. But, if a concept should be purposefully viewed in terms of its supporting imagery, it can be experienced openly in terms of its properties, rather than as a closed definitional unit. Albeit that it must be understood in such a case that the properties remain under definitional control, until they are deliberately altered in the interest of forming a new concept. In this latter way, a concept may be made available for formation into other concepts.

It can thus be seen that a reasoning process must break down into concept generation at various points. Were this not the case, the reasoning would become sterile. It would only produce what is known. For, though such a process were capable of linking many concepts together systematically, collectively they would mean nothing other than what they had meant individually.

A similar, but much freer, creative process takes place in an imaginative state of reverie, which involves an uninhibited flow of unregulated images. But an imaginative state of reverie only produces images. It does not convert them into concepts. Whereas, when the process occurs in a train of reason, it is carried out by means of the use of the regulated images within concepts. It proceeds by treating a concept as open. The images are then imaginatively rearranged, adding or removing some as properties specifically for the purpose of generating a new concept. The new concept will then take its place within the flow of reason.

New concepts not directly reflecting experience, but created imaginatively from properties encountered in experience, may be included among other concepts which are directly reflective of experience. In this way, inductive observation is "filled in" where gaps in understanding may have occurred. In such a way, concepts of energy relations have been deduced. It is by this means that a systematic discipline is developed.

Thus a science is not entirely a direct interpretation of experience. Rather, it is a controlled interpretation, in which individual elements are brought into unity with one another in order to create an integrated whole. However, due not only to changes in the facts of observation, but to the necessary generalizations and additions from imagination which are characteristic of such a process, the discipline is periodically subject to revision.

There are two orders of concepts: empirical and universal. Empirical concepts are those which express experiential facts which are gleaned from observation. These may be supplemented by imaginative concepts the properties of which are also drawn from observation. Universal concepts are those which create an independent generalization from facts.

To speak of Socrates as a particular man, or to speak of a number of particular individuals, is to utilize empirical concepts. Though there may be some generalization in the latter case, if the emphasis is on the number rather than on the individuals. Nevertheless, so long as it is a plurality, it relates directly to experience.

To speak of Bigfoot, or Sasquatch, is both imaginative and empirical. For the properties of this creature are both human and simian. But to speak generally of "humankind" is

The Thinking Process

to employ a universal concept. This universal does not relate directly to experience because no one has ever encountered a humankind. To create a universal concept like "humankind," one must extract certain common characteristics from known individuals and be confident of applying them to any person who might possibly be encountered.

49. The Structure of a Thought

A thought must not only be temporally but spatially limited. So it is only a partial truth to say that, when a physical entity is represented within a thought, it is contained within a temporally limited thought extension. For the durance of the thought is not the durance of the thing thought about. Nor is the spatial extension of the thought identical with that of the thing thought about. The thing thought about has its own temporal and spatial character.[43]

The thought has an object. It is the thing thought about. And that thing exhibits spatial extension. So the fact that it is a spatial extension implies physical limitation, which must be represented by the thought. This is why a thought, which

---

[43] This is, of course, the representational view, in which a distinction is assumed to exist between a physical object and its mental representation, any one mental representation being an abstraction from the physical, somewhat reduced in qualities or properties. Were the immaterial view to be entertained, the representation is the object. However, multiple representations may be assumed to collectively fill out the details of an object, thus providing the presumed physical object with differing mental representations, as in the representational view.

in fact does represent physical limitation, is said to occupy mental space. But mental space is not identical to physical space.

The mental space of the representation roughly corresponds to the physical space of the thing represented. But it is only a correlation. A mental space is not a physical space. It is a representation of physical space. Because thought extensions are not concurrent with one another in the manner in which physical extensions are contiguous in space, they do not physically limit one another. Rather, they occur sequentially. One thought limits another by replacing it. So this is the principal means by which a thought expresses limitation. A thought is temporal in character.

For this reason, the spatial limits of any physical object of thought are subsumed under the temporal limits of the thought and appear not to exist as spatial limits within that thought. The thought only represents spatial limits when specifically called upon to do so by a deliberate consideration of the object's overall physical character.

In other words, when a consideration of the object's physical character is entertained, the object is thoroughly realized as an image. It is realized in such a manner that the image is not overshadowed by conceptual limitations, such as a definition. But, if the image is in support of a concept, it is a shadow image.

This shadow image momentarily emerges in full realization. The mind carries out this task for the purpose of juxtaposing two objects within a sequence of two thoughts. The sequence makes them appear as if they were one thought. This is done so that one object may delimit the other

The Thinking Process

and thereby expose the spatial character of the object under consideration.

Say a person should think of a kitchen cabinet. By definition, it is a cupboard designed to hold cups, glasses, bowls, dishes, etc. This object, when entertained by the mind in the form of a concept, occupies mental space only by a faint suggestion of the set of images which define the concept. So no spatial element is brought under consideration. It is felt to be present without being exhibited. For the concept involves a physical object, which is something that occupies space.

But, if that object is called forth in a person's mind as a physical representation, then it is displayed in her mind, not as a concept, but as a fully realized set of images. And in this representation, it is limited by the proximity of other objects. Thus it is viewed in its spatial finitude.

In a thought, spatial extension is subordinate to temporal extension. For a thought is essentially a temporally limited phenomenon. And the thing thought about is represented within that temporally extended entity, the thought, and not always overtly so, if its spatial limitations are not emphasized.

Nevertheless, though not identical to it, the spatial limits of the object of a thought do correspond to the spatial limits of the thought. The sense of spatial limitation either concerns the thing thought about. Or it concerns the thought itself. Thus the spatial limitation of a thought—its occupation of mental space—is always understood by the mind. For the mental space of a thought is brought about by the object of the thought.

Thoughts occupy mental space because, either directly or indirectly, they express objects which are physically extended. Even with abstract concepts this is the case, though the extension pertains to the shadow images supporting the concept. Thus, if the thought is not seen to occupy mental space in accordance with something thought about, it is felt to do so in the sense that the thought itself is understood to occupy mental space.

A spatial extension is not experienced within a single thought in the way it is understood to be experienced in physical space. For something to occupy mental space as a thought is not the same as for it to occupy physical space. The thought is an image or a concept supported by images. It is a mental representation of the object thought about, not a physical equivalent of it. So the spatial extension of the thing thought about is merely understood within the thought, even when an image of an extended object is directly exhibited within the thought.

So the thought and the object thought about, as it exists within the thought, are both spatially extended in one sense alone: the thought represents an object which is physical, or which at least references physical properties conceived to be extended in some manner. In other words, just as the object thought about exhibits the characteristics of a spatially finite physical extension, so the thought of it is a representation in the mind of something which is physically and spatially extended.

Both are also extended temporally. And, if the thought should be said to be temporally extended because it represents something which is temporally extended, this is not a correlation. For the temporal extension of the thought may differ widely from that of the object thought about. This is, of course, in the sense of the thought representing something

The Thinking Process

individually thought about, as opposed to something conceived within its context of spatial change.

The latter type of representation follows objective parameters, including those of a temporal extension involving a series of thoughts. But the former is subjective and differs from them, the object being withdrawn from its dynamic physical context and entertained separately as an isolated object of thought. So both this thought and its source object are limited by temporal means, but not in the same way.

An object which is extended in physical space is temporally limited within a context of change. It supersedes another object and is replaced by yet another. Thoughts are limited by other thoughts in a similar manner. In either case, the presence of the object or thought is replaced by another which limits it in time. So, if thoughts parallel a physical activity, they are temporally conditioned by it.

But the existence of an object observed in a context of physical space may endure for a longer or shorter period than that of a thought about the same object entertained in disregard of such a context or in some sense in which the context is modified. So there is no temporal correspondence between them.

Yet this object is physically limited. And here there is a correspondence between the representation and the object. Either the thought indirectly represents the spatial extension of the object by simply recognizing itself as occupying mental space while exhibiting the object without concern for its properties. Or it directly represents the spatial extension of the object by means of images which demonstrate its extension.

So, in its act of spatial representation, the thought must either do one or both. For it will at least recognize itself as spatially extended in representing an object without emphasis upon the object's extension. Or it may specifically recognize the object as extended as well. The latter type of recognition is not a consequence of the former. Rather, it is a consequence of the thought's representation of the object's spatial extension, in which case the thought recognizes itself as extended precisely because it is representing the spatial extension of an object.

Therefore, either the thought understands itself to occupy mental space without overtly representing physical space. Or it must extend its object within itself. In the latter case, the thought understands itself to occupy mental space by means of its representation of the physical extension of the thing thought about.

On a final note, it may be recalled that a role for language was previously indicated. Language does play a role in thought organization. But, if it is assumed that the language passing through a person's mind is all that is the thought, this is an illusion. The language represents a superficial layer.

Beneath its sounds, sound sequences, and syntactical structure are individual images. And there are the interrelated properties of concepts which are represented by images. These determine the thought, not the language in which the thought appears to take place. For language is structured according to a different set of rules than those of association and logic. It does not render thought possible. It facilitates communication.

The Thinking Process

50. Mental Dynamics

Since thoughts are sequential, they are principally limited in a temporal manner. Whereas physical objects are limited contiguously as well as sequentially. Thus one thought is temporally limited when it is replaced by another thought. But, though the object within a thought is one which potentially exhibits spatial limitation, the thought containing it does not spatially preclude another thought. It limits it only on the basis of a shifting of mental focus. Consequently, a thought overtly represents spatial limitation only when called upon to do so. At all other times, the spatial character of its content is assumed. This is what is meant by mental space.

However, a person is not confined to thinking only about finite physical objects like stones, which have fully determinate characteristics. He can think about something partaking of both determinate and indeterminate characteristics, like an unending count of numbers. And this mixture of determinacy and indeterminacy stands midway between that which is delineable in finite terms and that which is not.

For example, when contemplating an unending count of numbers a person's thought is lacking in certain properties of physical experience. For the properties of physical experience are those of a completely determinate finitude. And the unending property of these numbers is indeterminate. But even such a thought as this is material in two ways.

It is material inasmuch as it is a thought and thus an extension of the mind expressing duration. And it is material insofar as it contains mental impressions, i.e., those informing the property "extension" which characterizes the arithmetical units of the numbers. For arithmetical units are extended.

Nevertheless, it remains immaterial in the unlimited character of its count. For, in spite of its reference to the material properties of number, there is no example in physical experience to support its indeterminacy. So, though it has a definition, the concept of an unlimited count of numbers floats in the mind in search of images to ground its unlimited count. Consequently, the ideal concept of an unending count of numbers must be considered immaterial.

All abstraction toward the condition of thought exhibits at least one nonfinite characteristic. It does so even when a person thinks about finite objects. For, when he thinks about a finite object, such as a stone, he apprehends the mental impressions of its qualities within a focused framework. He thinks it as a unity.

The mental impressions are finite. And focus forms them into an extension of thought, which is also finite. But the unity governing the process is consciousness, which is infinite. So all thoughts are differentiated in some degree from their content, even when that content only contains demonstrable physical references. Thus even a thought of a stone exhibits an immaterial characteristic. But this only concerns its relationship with the conscious mind.

In regard to an ideal concept, the content of the thought is not wholly physical. Thus it has no immediate reference but itself. For at least some of the properties informing its supporting imagery do not correlate to anything in physical experience. They are at best negative concepts, as when a string of counting numbers is defined as *not* ending.

The Thinking Process

Yet, in spite of this, the concept is recognizable in imagination in terms of its images because mental impressions must be involved as qualities in at least some of its properties, if the thought's object is to be envisioned at all. And these impressions, as well as the mental extension of the thought, are finite. Thus any thought is sufficiently material to be experienced as a thought.

All mental impressions can be encountered in the material realm. They are what they are. Only their associations within properties may differ. Consequently, all thoughts may be understood to access physical experience in varying degree. Accordingly, ideal concepts are not pure fabrications of the mind.

Even when a thought is expressed entirely in negative terms, such as is the case with the concept of consciousness, the terms reference mental impressions. In an attempt to delineate what consciousness is not, they collate properties which do not pertain to it. So, although ideal concepts inevitably reference physical properties in some way, they do not always do so in a positive manner. And what is not positive is not demonstrable. Thus the indeterminate property of unendingness in an unending count of numbers cannot be adduced, not even in imagination.

The fact that some thoughts access but do not match up to physical experience is telling. For it is in this sense that the following can be asserted. First, all empirical thoughts are thoughts of immediate physical reference. As such, they are direct or indirect abstractions from the physical. And what is meant by the term "indirect" is that some of these thoughts are derived from other thoughts, the latter thoughts being direct abstractions from the physical.

But secondly, an idealization, like that of an unending count of numbers, is different. It is only derived from physical experience inasmuch as it employs mental impressions—in this case, those qualities informing the property of extension in its arithmetical units, which in turn compose its numbers.

For an unending count of numbers is an invention involving the creation of an unaccustomed property: the fact that it is unending. So it is something which may be said to be arbitrarily composed. Consequently, it bears a unique form to which nothing physical correlates. Which is to say, an ideal concept is a thought extension after its own kind.

So any concept is an abstraction from the physical inasmuch as it has recognizable qualities. But the concept may also exhibit properties which exist only by suggestion. That is, they have no positive correlation to experience. Thus an ideal concept involves properties which cannot be experienced in imagination.

51. General, Universal, and Ideal

How is it that the mind creates a conceptualization which is not a direct representation of the physical, yet is still a thought? To understand this, let a thought which is universal rather than ideal be examined first. A concrete thought about a specific person would be the simplest form of thought. For it is a direct reference to the physical. As such, it is empirical. A person is a specific object. So the thought concerning

The Thinking Process

her is not derived from another thought. And, since the thought's reference is specific, its immediate representation is not a generalization.

But let a mental shift toward the universal be made by way of generalization. A reference can be made to a nonspecific plurality of persons—i.e., to people. Such a general concept would not reference all persons. Rather, it would indicate an unspecified number of people, not necessarily including all people.

A universal concept like "humankind," on the other hand, would emphasize properties common to all people, leaving aside those properties which are not common. The common properties would represent what is physically, behaviorally, and mentally characteristic of all people.

The definition based on these characteristics is established by means of a lifting of the common properties from numerous, but not all, instances of the object in question. At some point a sufficient number of people would be reached, so that it would be assumed those people not encountered would nevertheless fall under the definition.

The definition is then held by convention. So it is by convention that "humankind" would be assumed to fulfill the requirements of its definition. As a result, an examination of any undiscovered person who might be supposed to be encountered must also be supposed to support the definition. If not, the newly encountered object would not be considered to be a person, however much she resembled one.

It is in this way that such a concept would become universal. It is a defined generalization emphasizing only those properties found to be common to all objects which are to be recognized as members of humankind. This would appear to resemble the general concept "people." For any one of these people must be recognized by her properties. But there is a difference.

The difference is that the concept "humankind" is indeterminate in reference—i.e., it does not refer to any specific object. It is concerned neither with a single person, a multiple of people, nor people in general. Rather, without indicating specific persons, it refers to an indeterminate number of them, any one of whom is found in material experience. But the whole of the reference is not.

When people are referred to in this universal manner as humankind, no object or multiple of objects can be adduced from experience as a focus of the concept. For there is no such thing as a humankind. So the referent, being an unenumerated whole, and therefore indeterminate, is not finite. It is immaterial. For all material entities are finite. Which is to say, they are determinate.

Yet, though a universal concept is immaterial, it is not invented. Consequently, it is not ideal. So, clearly, if a universal concept is immaterial in reference, which is also true of an ideal concept, it must be distinguished from the ideal by this fact that there is nothing about it which is invented. Whereas there is something about the ideal concept which is invented.

A perfect circle is ideal. It is invented because its absolutely uniform circumference cannot be discovered in the material realm. For this reason, it is to be distinguished from each of the many physical circles which can only serve as its partial referents. Whereas a member of humankind is not to be distinguished from any specific person. For, as members of humankind, they are alike.

The Thinking Process

A perfect circle has a definition which requires multiple referents, no one of which fulfills its character. And a general concept, like "people," refers to an unspecified number of people which does not necessarily involve all people. The universal concept "humankind," on the other hand, exhibits a definition which applies to each and all of its appropriate referents, but to none in particular. Every person—no person being omitted—is a member of humankind. Thus "humankind" is neither an ideal nor a general concept.

An ideal concept can be quantified as singular. There is but one of its kind. One perfect circle is indistinguishable from others, insofar as it is a perfect circle. The different sizes of a perfect circle do not arise from its definition. By definition, there is but one perfect circle. Conversely, there are many referents to a universal which fulfill its universal character. But the number of these is undetermined. They cannot be quantified.

Now a general concept represents necessary as opposed to accidental properties. For it recognizes no distinction between tall and short people. This is also the case with a universal concept. But the general concept does not place an emphasis on properties. Rather, it is on the object. In other words, the focus of a general term is not upon its definition. It is upon a multiple of individual people.

This is how it differs from a universal concept. For a universal concept is specifically focused upon its definition. It raises the question, what is a member of humankind? It emphasizes the fact that it is a complete abstraction from particular experience. In being universal, it must, like a general concept, be considered on the basis of what it represents in experience. But what it represents is not a multiple of persons, but their essential properties. These become more important than the thing represented. For they are the defini-definition. And it is the definition, not the thing, which is paramount.

Any properties which are peculiar to one person as opposed to another are accidental. Consequently, they are excluded from consideration in either a general or universal reference. Yet this exclusion is not for the purpose of inventing a concept, as would be the case with the ideal, where, for example, irregularities in the curvature of a circumference are left out of the definition of a perfect circle. Rather, it is the normal exclusion of nonessential properties which is found in any general or universal term.

Because a universal concept is based on an emphasis upon its definition—it is entirely unspecific in application. Any person fulfills the definition of humankind. But it applies to all people, not to one alone or to some people. And its focus is upon what defines them. So, as a thought applying to no object in particular, it is outside physical time and place. It is immaterial in the sense that it exists only as a thought.

Each physical example which might be applied to a universal concept as a referent is determinate and does not express universality, though in its essential properties it is a full representation of the concept. But, since a universal concept refers to an indeterminate number of these referents, it is undecided in particularity. Thus a universal concept exhibits a character of independence. For it is removed from its referents, as is an ideal concept. But it is not definitionally independent of those referents, as is the case with an ideal concept.

The Thinking Process

52. Logic and the Intuitions

Logic is shaped by the same two intuitions as shape images and concepts. These are unity and plurality (totality being an application in which both are working together). No image, concept, or logical relation is formed without them. For example, take the syllogism:[44]

> All liars are fools.
> Some people are liars.
> Therefore, some people are fools.

This is one of the valid moods into which syllogistic reasoning naturally falls. Within each of its statements, concepts supply the subject and predicate terms.

What the mind apprehends in each statement is a juxtaposition or separation of concepts. This is brought about by the intuitions of unity and plurality. For, where there is a complete convergence of meaning, as in the case of a subject and predicate being united under the universal quantifier "all," there is a unity. And, where there is a complete divergence of meaning, as under the universal quantifier "no," there is a disunity, or a plurality. This distinction between unity and plurality is what is meant by a juxtaposition or separation of concepts.

---

[44] A few simple principals of Aristotelian logic are employed in this discussion. But the implications are broader. For the intuitions form the basis of all thinking.

In the former case the subject and predicate are combined in a singleness of meaning. In the latter there is more than one meaning. For, while the subject and predicate are equated under the "all," they are disjunct under the "no." On the other hand, where the existential quantifiers "some" and "some...not" are employed, there is only a partial junction or a partial disjunction in meaning. Both of these constitute pluralities. For they represent a combination of inclusion and exclusion of meaning which provides a distinction between concepts.

These circumstances occur in the following ways. Initially, the subject and predicate of a proposition are self-contained concepts. Thus they function independently, until they are brought under the influence of a quantifier. The purpose of a quantifier is to distribute their meanings in accordance with the inclusiveness or exclusiveness of the overall statement.

For example, the subject and predicate of the first premise of the syllogism above have a relationship of unity. This is because, under the influence of the universal quantifier "all," liars are held to be equivalent to fools. Thus the subject and predicate express identical meanings. This does ignore the possibility that, in a broader context, not all fools may be liars. But such a possibility is left unstated. In the proposition, liars and fools are equated. For the proposition is not concerned with any other possibility.

This means that the expression of either concept, "liars" or "fools," assumes identical properties with the other. Liars exhibit the character of fools. And fools exhibit the character of liars. For, in spite of the divergence of their original defi-

The Thinking Process

nitions, the two concepts are held in a relationship of identity.

So what appeared in the original subject and predicate to be distributed properties are now the same under the quantifier "all." They are shared within the logical context of the statement, which determines the meaning of its terms for the duration of their use within it. And, in fact, since nothing more broadening is asserted about fools within the syllogism, the situation is maintained for its duration.

In the second premise of the syllogism, the existential quantifier "some" causes the meaning of the predicate "liars" to make up only a part of the meaning of the subject "people." For the concept "people" is separated into "some people" who are liars and those who are not. Consequently, while the subject and predicate are made to share meaning to some extent, they are not identical.

Now, in consideration of the fact that liars and fools express a single meaning in the first premise, this meaning makes up a part of the concept "people." But it is only a part of it. For only some people are liars and fools. Others are not. Thus there is a plurality of concepts in both the second premise and concluding statement of the syllogism.

For these reasons, all three terms ("people," "liars," and "fools") can be recognized as being compared according as they agree or disagree with a whole or a part of one another. Or, to state this alternately, the terms are compared in three ways: according to an identical meaning of the concepts, according to a complete divergence in meaning, or according to a partial identity and partial difference in meaning.

When the concepts are considered to be identical, they are in unity. They are one concept, insofar as the statement containing them is concerned. Where there is a partial distinction in meaning within a concept, as in the subject "people" of both the second premise and the conclusion, only a portion of the concept is united in meaning with "liars" and "fools." A part of the subject is not united with these predicates. So there is a plurality of meaning within the statements.

Moreover, were the first premise different, it could have been the case that "no liars are fools." If that were so, then the two concepts, "liars" and "fools," would have been completely dissociated. This would express a conceptual plurality. Or, if the second premise had been "some people are not liars," it would have clearly suggested that "some people *are* liars." So a partial dissociation between two versions of the subject would occur, resulting in a plurality of meaning.

Thus it can be seen that it is by means of different types of association and differentiation between various subjects and predicates that the intuitions of unity and plurality shape conceptual life. And, as demonstrated elsewhere in this work, it is by these means as well that they effect the development of individual thought images and the concepts they support. Consequently, in facilitating association and differentiation, the intuitions play a ubiquitous role in thought.

The Thinking Process

53. The Structure of Reason

All attempts at either a material or an ideal explanation of logic have failed hitherto because either approach taken individually falls short of grasping the origin and importance of the intuitions of unity, plurality, and totality. Without these intuitions, the powers of abstraction, of verbal and mathematical classification, of conceiving the arithmetical unit (the number 1), and of logical deduction could not be accounted for.

Yet the origin of these intuitions can be discovered in experience. It is the unity of consciousness. Since consciousness is unextended, indivisible, and unbounded in character, its experience is unity. It is a unity without extension, division, or limitation. This experience of unity is thus the source of the first intuition: the intuition of unity. It's expression is a fundamental function of the mind. That is, because the intuition is derived from consciousness, it is prior to any activity of the mind. So the experience of unity becomes the intuition of unity. And it is this intuition which delineates material awareness.

Both the recognition of a material unity and a recognition of its limitation are accomplished by means of adjustments of mental focus to greater and lesser fields of consciousness. Thus material experiences are limited by other material experiences, one act of focus being opposed to another. And this becomes a ground for the second intuition, plurality. From this it can be seen that the second intuition is derived from the first. For it is material unities which are recognized in contradistinction to one another. So, if the experience of consciousness is the ground of the intuitions, focus is their mechanism.

To fix mental focus upon material experience is to engage that experience with attention. To shift mental focus to another experience is to recognize both experiences as limited. Thus it is to recognize one object, or set of objects, among others. The broadening of mental focus is a shifting of attention within the field of consciousness. This results in a prior focus upon a single object or small number of objects being made to enclose a broader field.

Both states of focus are acts of one consciousness. They are a shifting of attention to different experiences. An individual act of focus is thus an imposition of unity upon a field of material experience, regardless of the number of entities involved. For this reason, the act of mental focus is always an expression of unity. For it is the same unified consciousness shifting its attention relative to its content.

Thus experience is folded within itself: it is experience within experience—consciousness of something within consciousness of a greater content. For consciousness can alter the range of its focus, enlarging or diminishing its content. It can recognize a single object as a unity. Then it can enlarge its field to encounter a plurality: one object among others.

In addition, the mind's ability to narrow or broaden its focus makes possible the exercise of a third intuition: totality. For, if unity and limitation (plurality) construct a world, the intuition of totality, which is derived from a combined exercise of the first two, provides the power of thought. This is the ability to form images and concepts.

The Thinking Process

Thought occurs when the intuition of unity is applied to mental impressions associated together in varying ways. In other words, thought involves flexible focus. The objects of that focus are individual mental impressions and associations of mental impressions. Both of these provide instances of limited unity. The recognition of more than one unity establishes the intuition of plurality. The power of recognizing pluralities of units as independent of one another in unity is the intuition of totality.

So consciousness is both a general awareness and a specific field of awareness. The general awareness is consciousness embracing its entirety of content. A specific field of awareness is a division of this content. To put it another way, unity is what is being exercised in any act of mental focus. This unity can be defined as consciousness alone, without reference to its content. It can also be defined in terms of an entirety of content. And it can be identified in terms of a single mental impression, an association of impressions, or an array of objects made up of those impressions.

In each case, mental focus is either a unity. Or it is making one. When making a unity, it is drawing focused-upon content into the character of its own unity. Perhaps two mental impressions are being focused upon. Perhaps three, and then four, and five. Perhaps more. Thus the mind experiences not only a single entity or a plurality of them. It can experience multiple pluralities.

When multiple pluralities are recognized, this is an exercise of the third intuition, totality. It is through the third intuition that the mind is able to recognize one plurality apart from other pluralities, as when it distinguishes between four and five. For a totality of five is different than that of four.

The mind experiences mental impressions as individual units mutually limiting one another. Or it experiences objects composed of those impressions in the same way. It combines this with a recognition that these mutually limiting impressions or objects are gathered together in a unity. So the experience of impressions or objects mutually limiting one another results in an exercise of the intuition of plurality. And a further recognition that these mutually limiting impressions or objects can be gathered together in a unity is an additional exercise of the intuition of unity. Thus the two intuitions, unity and plurality, operating together constitute a third intuition: totality.

So a totality is a plurality held within a focus of unity. And in the case of an object (which is a unity of properties individually made up of a unity of mental impressions), a totality is the experience of a unity of unities. It is these three intuitions—unity, plurality, and totality—which facilitate the powers of abstraction, concept formation, the development of the arithmetical unit (the number 1), and logical deduction.

Because mathematics is almost entirely independent of physical experience, perhaps it could be said that the establishment of the arithmetical unit is the most striking of these mental processes. For it cannot be derived from any specific entity in physical experience. It is an idealization.

Its only relationship with a physical experience is the fact that the associated mental impressions of any physical object constitute an extension. And an arithmetical unit is an extension. But it is an extension without discernible qualities. In

The Thinking Process

other words, it is an abstraction from physical extension. So the abstract conception of the arithmetical unit is that of extension alone without the direct support of imagery, as paral-paralleled, for example, by the kindred geometrical figure of a line. For neither are the properties of a line discernible. It has no breadth. So it is also an ideal concept.

These are among the extremes of abstraction. Mathematical rules of context alone define an arithmetical unit. For it must be uniform throughout. That is, it must be identical to and indistinguishable from any other unit. The single exception to this definitional limitation is the fact that it may vary in magnitude according to context. In other words, it may be a 1 in one place and a 1/10 of that 1 in another.

Now the general process of concept formation begins with a gathering up and segregating of mental impressions by means of mental focus. These associated impressions are united in an image. A few impressions can form an image of an individual property. Then, by means of a definition, certain salient properties are selected for emphasis from a number of combined properties. In this way, a concept is produced.

The process begins with mental impressions regarded as physical. These are the qualities of an object of thought which directly represents physical experience. But any representation is in the mind. This is true of a direct image of physical experience. Otherwise, the experience would not occur.

So an imagined image produced from the properties of previous physical images would characterize an independently constructed thought. The impressions held in the mind as the content of the original physical images would have been the ones directly exhibiting physical impressions.

Thus physical objects, which are composed of properties, and these in turn of qualities, are experienced as mental objects. But mental objects may or may not represent physical objects. For they can be works of imagination which recombine physical properties in new ways. Accordingly, the mind's various images of circles represent physical experience. But the concept of a perfect circle departs from it.

So mental impressions initially entertained as physical qualities brought together in a perceptual image can inform many of the properties which make up a concept. But the properties of the concept are not necessarily identical to the properties of physical representations. Thus they become the matter of independent concepts, like perfect circles, which have many of the properties of physical circles, but differ from them in having the property of a uniform curvature of the circumference. This last is a property which cannot be encountered in physical experience. So it is posited as being what is not experienced. But other imagined concepts may simply be recombinations of physical properties, such as the concept of a unicorn.

A concept is a thought composed of images. It is these which play a shadow role supporting the properties of its verbal definition. So, since a thought is based on imagery, and the imagery is made up of qualities, any thought can be mined for its qualities in making another thought. For the qualities are the mental impression content which is needed in the formation of images, and therefore of all thoughts.

The qualities of an object are mental impressions, whether the object be considered in physical terms or as an object of

The Thinking Process

thought. The mental impressions can either make up a physical object or not. So such thoughts as are imaginatively derived from other thoughts will be more or less distant in character from the original representations of physical objects which supplied a fundamental expression of qualities. In other words, they may exhibit different associations of qualities in terms of properties, as is demonstrated by the distinction in properties between a material circle and a perfect circle.

So concept formation can involve images composed of qualities which are understood to represent an immediate experience of physical objects. Or a concept may be drawn from images held in memory. These memory images may represent physical properties or objects. Or they may be distinctly different from them.

In the latter case, the images may become the supporting properties of concepts which are imagined but not encountered in physical experience. Or they may become the supporting properties of concepts which are ideal in character, like the concepts of mathematics. In any case, the final result of this process is a concept, whether it be supported by images representative of physical experience, or whether it be supported by images restructured in their qualities.

If an image is to be included in a process of reasoning, the image must represent a supporting property of a concept because it is the fixed properties of a concept which are rendered reliable for effective logical transitions of thought. The image becomes a closed property. For an image is an open thought when it has variable qualities. The images of a concept are closed because its properties do not exhibit variable qualities. A concept has defined properties composed of qualities which are made invariable for the sake of consistency in expression.

Now, in moving from images to the development of a concept, where the images are fixed as properties by a definition, the building of that concept can be understood to occur in stages. It may begin with an induction of properties from physical experience. In such a case, the representations of physical properties, which are initially apprehended as images of perception, would be subsequently recognized as images held independently in the mind. By this means, their constituent qualities would be made available for possible reorganization into new imagery as properties.

But concepts are derived from images previously stored in memory, as their development is deliberative. So these images will already either have become new creations or will have originated and been retained as representations of perception. So there is either new image formation or the use of perceptual images as they are. These can be used in any combination.

As indicated, it is a definition which gathers images into a concept. The definition translates independent imagery into the supporting imagery of a concept. In other words, it converts it into properties. These properties are definitionally expressed in language, thus concealing the imagery behind words. But it is nevertheless the imagery which both forms and moves concepts through the mind, not the overlay of language, which conceals the underlying process.

The Thinking Process

54. Qualities, Properties, and Concepts

Due to their multiplicity within objects or the properties of objects, individual mental impressions are generally obscured. For these are qualities. And a specific combination of qualities is what constitutes an object or a property of an object. Whereas other combinations make up other objects or properties of objects.

But within a specific object or property, unless its qualities are singled out for scrutiny, it is not always clear where one quality ends and another begins, since qualities, as mental impressions, are individually unextended. For it is only in combination that they are extended and recognized as an object or a property of an object.

What is being noted in particular is the fact that a plurality of mental impressions within a property is a blending which often obscures distinctions. Thus it is the same concerning an object, insofar as its qualities are concerned. For the obscuring of qualities in terms of properties is an obscuring of them in the object.

But between properties or objects the situation is otherwise. For an image represents either a property or a compound of properties, which latter is an object. In either case, the property or object constitutes a distinct object of a thought. And there can only be one object of a single thought. So thought images do not blend together.

Thus images exhibiting identical properties remain individualized when held in association. Each is distinct. Rather, there is a sequential development of individual thoughts, each exhibiting an image. So, to obtain a plurality of objects of thought, a grouping must be made. This grouping becomes a set of objects of thought, each a distinct image.

These images remain uncombined in order to avoid obscuring their individual characteristics. Consequently, when they are brought together as properties in support of a concept, they cannot be a blend. For each image posits its own character, its individuality being set off from others. Thus there is a distinct plurality of these.

In this way, a union of several images held in association within a concept becomes a grouping of thoughts which is presented sequentially in the mind. It is this sequence which must be opposed to another as a separate concept. For this concept is plural in terms of thoughts, insofar as its apprehension in terms of images is concerned. So, within the bounds of a grouping of properties, such a concept exhibits a plurality of thoughts, or images.

Each group is thus a totality of images representing properties, each of them as a separate thought. For the concept can only be a single thought when it is expressed in terms of a verbal definition. Whereas, if the supporting images are called forth, they must emerge as separate thoughts.

Note that, when a sense of limitation concerning anything is being created in the mind, there is always an associative act involved in forming a contrast between one thing and another. It is an opposition. This is what takes place when a concept is considered in terms of its imagery, as opposed to when it is considered in terms of its definition, or verbal expression.

In other words, when verbally expressed, as opposed to being expressed as a set of images, a concept is a single

The Thinking Process

thought extension exhibiting temporal limits. Its temporal limits distinguish it as one thought as opposed to another. This is its bounded character, which is what makes it material.

The temporal limits act as boundaries when a verbal contrast is required in making a distinction between thoughts. One verbal concept can be held up against another as they appear in sequence before the mind. It is this which gives a verbal concept its material integrity: it is bound by other verbal concepts.

So a verbal concept isolates itself from another as a separate and complete extension of thought. For it is a classification. This is made clear by its definition, which verbally distinguishes it from other concepts. The distinction, of course, refers to its properties. But these are supported by a plurality of images, which are a plurality of thoughts. Whereas the verbal concept constitutes one thought.

A verbal classification expresses a limited unity, or focus of the mind, concerning, but not exhibiting, certain properties. The properties are brought under the intuition of plurality. But, unlike them, qualities lose their individual identity in varying degree. Thus, in terms of its qualities, as opposed to its properties, a concept is an indivisible unity. This functions in support of the verbal integrity of the concept. But the properties of the concept remain a plurality.

The complexities of concept formation are made possible through the intuitions of unity, plurality, and totality. Thus a concept is a unity, a plurality, and a totality. It is a unity when considered as an independent thought verbally expressed. It is also a unity in terms of its qualities. But it is a plurality in terms of the diversity of its properties. And the grouping of these is a totality.

55. Consciousness and Its Content

The mind initially experiences itself as an unlimited unity. This is consciousness devoid of a consideration of its content. As such, it is not only unlimited, it is unextended and indivisible. But the mind also experiences the data of experience, which are mental impressions received within consciousness. This is its content.

The mind is aware that its consciousness and its content are integrated in one field of awareness. For together they constitute the whole of that awareness. But this comprehensive awareness alone, this recognition of the full range of experience without further elaboration, is a synthesis which provides no powers of analysis.

For analysis to occur, consciousness and its content must be separated, so that the one may operate upon the other. This is a separation of content from the original union of consciousness and content. Consciousness thus forms a relationship to its content. It not only experiences itself as a separate unity. It does so with intent.

For it employs its powers of focus to organize the data of its content. In other words, it moves its attention from one datum, or set of data, to another, experiencing each separately as a unity. It thus proceeds to employ its sense of unity as

The Thinking Process

an intuition, beginning by focusing upon the individual mental impressions which are its initial material content.

In this way, it exercises unity as belonging to its field of focus. Thus it recognizes each mental impression within that field as an independent entity. And, as it observes one mental impression as set off against another, it discovers multiple impressions within its field of focus. That is how it exercises its second intuition, the intuition of plurality.

So if each mental impression, like the color red or the taste of sweetness, is a differentiated entity, multiples of them can be associated in various ways according to mental focus as it is broadened and shifted among them. And, where there is a repeated presentation of associated physical impressions occurring independently of the will, physical objects and their properties are recognized. Thus the fundamentals of physical experience are laid down.

An independent intellectual interpretation of this initial experience follows. The interpretation is dependent upon the will.[45] Thus an articulation of mental impressions characterizes both perception and independent thought construction: the laying down of fundamental experience for perception, and the intellectual interpretation of it for thought. And the distinction between the two is not precise. For they are inextricably mixed.

Perception of physical experience occurs as images in the mind. However, these images are determined by the order of appearance of individual impressions, which is largely inde-

---

[45] Will is here understood to occur within a material context and not prior to its unfolding. It is thus being considered from a representational perspective.

pendent of the will.[46] This is different from concept formation, which is dependent upon the will. In fact, the latter may be said to be the goal of human intelligence. For the mind seeks to classify and define—in other words, to create order. This is to say that concept formation is the final, precise articulation of thought. It is what allows a person to reason, to predict, and to plan.

The mind originates its independent thought processes by grouping representational images under concepts which are intended to mirror material experience. These images represent physical objects or their properties. However, the mind recombines some of the properties to form imaginary concepts and modifies others to create ideal concepts. These enhance systematic thinking about material experience. Thus there is an increasingly subtle and complex conceptual overlay which organizes thought.

But, in the process of creating independent thought, the mind comes to experience itself in conflicting roles. As a unity, it experiences itself as unlimited and indivisible. But, having given its content an independent character, it also recognizes itself as content. For it discovers itself to be one among many centers of consciousness. Thus arises a sense of the materiality of human existence.

Hence the eternal human conflict between mind and body, spirit and matter. For a human being is at once awareness and aware of a world which includes himself. A paradox oc-

---

[46] In the manner of the representational perspective, some leeway may be allotted for the way in which an individual chooses to approach a physical object—e.g., top to bottom or bottom to top. Or perhaps a person notes color before shape or shape before color. Nonetheless, in such cases the properties of the object remain the same.

The Thinking Process

curs: human awareness encompasses the world, which world also encompasses human awareness. The world is in humanity. And humanity is in the world.

56. Logical Thinking

Though there may be an identity of some mental impressions between separate thoughts, the thoughts are dissimilar if not all their mental impressions are the same. They are independent of one another. Yet, beyond this distinguishing between the objects of thoughts, the images which represent these objects can lend themselves toward a subdivision and realignment of their content. So thoughts may be modified into other thoughts.

Or when this is not possible, as in the case of images bound within concepts, the concept can lend itself toward a recognition that its content matches, or might be assumed to match, a portion of the content of another concept. So an alignment of content in order to extend meaning can take place. For some properties from one concept can be brought into affinity, or be presumed to do so, with those of another. This is the process of logical association between concepts.

As a result of this capacity, the mind can place one concept, or classification, under the defining limits of another. The definition of the more inclusive classification will then act as a set of parameters governing the original classification. Thus more is known about a concept when it is placed under a definition which is more comprehensive than its own.

It is in this manner that classifications are nested, which means one is governed fully or in part by the other. Consequently, logic becomes a means of interrelating classifications. Though some of these relations may be disjunctive in character, as in the statements: "no *p* is *q*" or "some *p* is not *q*." In these latter cases, the original concept "*p*" is defined in a negative manner. All or some portion of the subject is understood as not included in the predicate. So it is a form of nesting by exclusion. Yet even in this case it provides a closer definition of the subject by the predicate.

Verbal classifications are less precisely interrelated than mathematical classifications because there is a more extensive reference to properties in the larger domain of material experience. This causes endless modifications of classifications which are not limited to quantitative comparisons. Thus there is no independent, inviolable set of rules to govern them, other than those which point up comparisons in meaning. Whereas mathematics follows rules of quantification.[47] And, though these are ultimately comparative, they are highly elaborated.

The material realm cannot be reduced to a complex set of abstractions unless it is brought under a restrictive discipline, such as when physical science is subsumed under mathematical rule. This is to say that, in its full experiential character,

---

[47] Projective geometry is most likely not an exception, though a transformational formula which would integrate all its variations has not been articulated. Such a formula would undoubtedly involve the infinitesimal calculus, due to the indeterminately minute integrations of change involved.

The Thinking Process

the material realm is not a system. For the more it is experienced, the more it evades thought. Conversely, the reason mathematics is such a precisely integrated system is that it belongs strictly within the realm of thought.

Philosophy falls short of such precision because, in its thinking (as opposed to its vision), it is not as ideal as mathematics. That is, its concepts cannot be referenced back to a concept devoid of all material content but that of extension, like, for example, the arithmetical unit (the number 1). For, other than its extension, the arithmetical unit exhibits immateriality. It is ideal.

On the other hand, every new philosophy begins with a unique perspective on material experience. That experience involves the full range of mental impressions available within the content of consciousness. Hence the perpetual arising of new or altered classifications and the philosophical systems derived from them. Philosophy is indeed ideal in this sense of continually expressing a new perspective, some of the unifying concepts of which must be invented to integrate the whole.

The sciences lie between the extremes of mathematics and philosophy, each separate field of investigation taking a different position, depending on how close to quantification the nature of its investigations is. Physics is more rigorously structured than evolutionary biology because it is predicated upon concepts like extension, motion, and energy, which are matters of proportion. Thus it is closer to mathematics.

As may be inferred from Hume's bifurcation of knowledge into "matters of fact"[48] and "relations of ideas,"[49] each science attempts to govern the unregulated realm of facts through their regulation by more rigorously defined ideas. This is particularly evident in physics, which increasingly attempts to explain material experience in mathematical terms. In so doing, it approaches, but does not quite reach, a condition characterized by rule without material content.

Such a thorough conversion of content into rule would threaten ordinary thinking. For it would remove itself from the full range of mental impressions available to experience. As it is, it seems odd, even bizarre, to common understanding. But its near approach to such a condition nevertheless produces results. This is because an explanation framed almost entirely in terms of rule—that is, a system attempting to be utterly limited to rigorous conditions of interrelation—renders material experience ever so close to the mind's reach toward a perfect order.

57. Fluid Classification

Let it be asserted that "all horses are Arabian horses." Let it then be stated that "some horses are not Arabian horses."

---

[48] David Hume, *An Enquiry Concerning Human Understanding*, Sect. IV, Part I, 21.
[49] David Hume, *An Enquiry Concerning Human Understanding*, Sect. IV, Part I, 20.

The Thinking Process

This is a logical contradiction. What has caused this? In the first statement, there is universal predication. Thus the classification "horses" is limited to the classification "Arabian horses," making the two terms identical in the properties they are assumed to encompass. But in the second statement the classification "horses" extends beyond the classification "Arabian horses." Thus both these statements cannot be true.

The terms are identical in the first statement because Arabian horses are a type of horse. Since, as a predicate term, they are being universally applied to the subject "horses," there can be no classification for "horses" which is not "Arabian horses." And, since Arabian horses are a type of horse, they are limited to the classification "horses." There are no Arabian horses which are not horses.

Now suppose that in support of this assertion a practical study is carried out. And it is found that all horses actually are Arabian horses. For a genetic determination indicates that the Arabian set of genes is simply that of the Equus caballus species. At this point, can it be said that nature would invariably substantiate the proposition, "all horses are Arabian horses"?

It cannot because the language can be altered through a change in its signification, due to a subsequent alteration in the facts of nature. For example, a modification could be made in what is meant by Equus caballus. Perhaps further research finds that the species has a broader gene pool than originally thought. So the classification "Equus caballus" can be extended in meaning to include factors previously ignored.

As a result, it is determined that Clydesdales are also horses. For the gene pool of "Equus caballus" has been broadened to include them. Now the proposition, "some horses are not Arabian horses," would be found to be true. And the statement, "all horses are Arabian horses," would be false.

In this way, it can be seen that no classification is absolute. For it is only a verbal concept. And physical fact is no more than a probability, however high. Thus the verbal concept is a flexible instrument of thought, which may be modified by a different signification. This makes it clear that, if individual concepts within a system of thought are flexible, the entire system is flexible as well.

That is, if a single term or proposition is subject to possible change, so will an entire theoretical system be subject to change. For concepts and propositions make up the system, just as qualities make up properties and properties a concept. In other words, a system can be regarded as a single classification. For its signification can be altered like that of a term or proposition, since its terms and propositions function in the manner of qualities and properties.

A theory (i.e., a system) would of course be composed of the logical interrelationships which characterize the individual concepts and propositions located within it. So, just as is the case with individual terms and statements, an entire scientific paradigm[50] can be exchanged for a new one by altering a pivotal element in, or a sufficient portion of, its signification.

One way it could be accomplished is by expanding the overall field of signification of the system. Thus it can be

---

[50] The term "paradigm" is used here in the sense indicated by Thomas Kuhn in *The Structure of Scientific Revolutions*.

The Thinking Process

seen that any theory composed of logically integrated classifications is vulnerable. In spite of the convincing firmness of empirical evidence at any point in time, the system's apparent inviolability is no more than a product of human will.

It is decided at some point that the system is complete. But human effort retains its capacity to enlarge its range of expectation in a manner which had not been previously considered. Thus the theory of relativity has enlarged the domain of classical physics, though it had once been thought complete. Due to an expanded reference, the overall structure of the science has been modified.

But what about physical experience? Does it not have an independent role in determining meaning? It does have such a role, but not logically. Initial physical experience is represented by mental imagery. Insofar as an image or a train of images is concerned, it is conditioned by mental impressions which are their foundational content. But concept formation and logical relations are not restricted to the original image associations of these impressions.

Neither classifications expressed within statements as terms, nor statements themselves, nor entire systems of statements constituting a theory are inherent in the foundations of experience. Thus what are transferred to thought as material experience are not the original representational images, but simply the mental impressions of which they are composed.

These can be arranged into concepts in close adherence to physical experience. Or they can be modified into concepts designed to fill gaps in empirical experience. In addition, they can be developed into concepts made to fit into a system which was constructed for reasons that originally had little to do with present research. Thus any thought system is not only affected by the pattern of signification which is adopted. The system itself may grow in ways which alter its general application. And that shift in overall meaning may not be noticed for some time.

Reasoning involves concepts and logical relations which not only reflect, but affect, the character of its signification. For reason is a deliberative form of mental structuring, which means it is a product of the will. So a theoretical structure may begin its factual reference in accordance with a specific set of standards for the formation of its individual concepts and propositions. Then these may change in their reference over time, due to the addition of other concepts and propositions which have been integrated into the system.

This may not be in entire agreement with experience. For, as a theoretical structure grows in the comprehensiveness of its application, it supersedes some of its original facts, since the accuracy of the system as a whole becomes more important than that of the elements which compose it. This distancing from direct experience arises from the fact that the intellect not only grows in its understanding. In its preoccupation with conceptual integration, it often becomes increasingly detached from direct experience.

But what is of interest is the fact that it is not the signification of content which is the principal means of determining the meaning of statements and systems. It is logical structure. As already indicated, the relationship between concepts is a fluid medium which transforms itself through a train of predications and entailments, where neologisms not only arise, but can come to play a vital role.

The Thinking Process

For it is frequently the case that names for things which are more imagination than fact must be invented to complete a system. In time, the newness of such concepts is forgotten. And they are accepted as indisputable fact. Yet they are often supported by very indirect experimental observations.

So what becomes a matter of concern is the manner in which these neologisms within a pattern of predications and entailments not only pass along new meanings, but in the process modify old ones. Thus, even if nothing were to be added to or subtracted from the overall referential content of most of the concepts involved, a shift in emphasis on the properties within them and the relations between those properties can occur.

58. Shared Meaning

Discussions in previous chapters of this work have been concerned with examining the character of individual classifications and how they partially or fully encompass one another. But there is another aspect of the fluid character of classification which involves the question, how are different levels of classification representative of a single meaning? For both a proposition and a theory can be understood as single concepts.

Just as the individual terms in a proposition are classifications, a proposition itself is a classification. It is a concept. Thus the statement, "some horses are not Arabian horses" is a concept. The same may be said for a system: a theory. All the propositions of the system are joined together in meaning to produce one overall meaning which can be summed up as a concept. As a result, the entire system becomes a classification—not in detail, of course, but in essence, or meaning.

Conversely, a proposition may be stated to define a term. Or a complex system of propositions could be developed in detailed explanation of a single proposition or term. For example, the statement "horses are either Arabian horses or Clydesdales" can be adduced to express the meaning of the concept "Equus caballus," this being followed by a theoretical discussion of genetic determinates demonstrating why it is so.

It is so because "Equus caballus," as understood in the context originally introduced in the previous chapter, includes both Arabians and Clydesdales and no others. So, since term, proposition, and system can be recognized as individual classifications which are equivalent in meaning (though not in detail), they are interchangeable. For their shared meanings point to common references.

Thus, where a system supports a proposition and the proposition supports a single concept, each expressing the same general meaning, the relationship of any one of these to the other two may be referred to as a special type of nesting of classifications: the system being equivalent to the proposition, and the proposition being equivalent to the concept. Only the extent of detail differs, not the meaning.

Inasmuch as it involves a nesting of classifications, this is not dissimilar to the previously explored relations between genus and species. But unlike genus and species, where the relationship between them would be one of partial identity of the latter with the former (other species also being included

The Thinking Process

in the genus), there is in the above case an interchangeable character. For a logically interrelated system of thought is at once an entire system of propositions, a single proposition, and a single term.

This illustrates the fact that, even should a term, proposition, and system differ in meaning, it is clear that each can be reduced to a single (albeit different) concept. And the reason this is important is that the mind is essentially a classifier—an enlarger or restrictor of meaning. It reasons by means of association, regardless of whether the process involves an inclusion or exclusion of properties. In other words, it always works under the principles of unity and plurality.

59. Logical Inference

The science of logic is founded upon associations and dissociations (which latter must be associated in order to be dissociated). So to create rational discourse, associations between concepts are made for the purpose of an inclusion of the meaning or partial meaning of one within the other. And dissociations are made in a similar manner for the purpose of an exclusion of the same. This process involves both a linking and an isolation of statements by comparison and inference. The following is the manner in which such discourse develops.

Dogs are warm-blooded, fur-bearing animals that nurture their young through lactation. So are cats. They can be associated in this respect. So the classification "mammals" is created in order to be inclusive of them both. Accordingly, a person may reason from dogs or cats or both to mammals, or from mammals to dogs or cats or both. Or she may reason from dogs to cats on the basis of the properties they share. That is, she may infer that properties belonging to these classifications are shared.

However, there is a flaw in assuming that logic is infallible. For it is thought to be so because association and dissociation appear to be infallible. This seems to be the case, even if the association or dissociation is made by assumption, rather than by a matching or differentiation of observed properties.

But it is an unstable foundation, since a thinker need only shift her focus to alter her inference. If she moves her emphasis to other properties, she changes the association or dissociation, however subtly. Consequently, she modifies the discourse. This may easily occur because, as a theoretical network of ideas is built up, the addition of new ideas can modify the meaning of those they join.

Thus it may be observed that a dog is a social animal, while most cats are not. It may be further noted that sociability is a classification that includes many birds. Thus dogs and waterfowl share an identity which most cats do not share with them. From this it can be seen that a predilection in deciding the relative importance of properties may influence the direction of discourse. For animal taxonomy might have been arranged on the basis of behavior rather than morphological or phylogenic characteristics. That it was not is a matter of convenience in taxonomic organization.

A claim is frequently made concerning mathematics that there is little or no required recourse to inductive inference in

The Thinking Process

its reasonings. The syntax of mathematics is thought to be freed from semantic interference. Consequently, mathematicians need not submit to the murky experience of the senses.

So there would appear to be nothing to alter the pattern of mathematical associations. For it is established by rules of convention, which are independent of observation (as in $4 = 4$, while $4 = 2$ twice and half of 8). However, once these relations are independently determined, they are applied to matters of observation.

The standard for this convention is the arithmetical unit (the number 1), which is an intellectual extension devoid of properties other than extension. But such a convention is a product of agreement and will. Agreement sets the standard. And will enforces it. So it is association alone which stands inviolate. As long as the properties forming an association are agreed upon, the association holds. For that is the mind's way of relating concepts.

But the agreement may vary, particularly when it concerns a physical reference. For imagination may group mental impressions in different ways within properties, thus altering the properties. And the properties within subjects and predicates affect their meaning and thus the distribution of meaning within logical statements. So the meaning of a statement can be subject to change.

This is also the case when associations or dissociations are made concerning properties which are assumed and not observed, as in "all philosophers are impecunious." And it is the case when properties are independent of physical reference. Thus even in arithmetic the base of ten—a fundamental property of contemporary arithmetical practice—is subject to substitution by something else.

George Lowell Tollefson

Experience does establish irrefutable sequences of mental impressions in the mind, which form the basic imagery of perception. But, while the fundamental stock of mental impressions for a particular perception remains the same, the object may be approached in different ways. In addition, it is not perception, but thought, which relates a person to her experience. For her understanding of her experience results from an intellectual interaction with it.

Many of her conceptual associations of properties are products of abstraction from initial experience. Thus they are in varying degree subject to imagination. Consequently, they are rendered at least partially independent of immediate experience, the perception of the original associations of experience having been altered.

They are set free in a manner in which those of immediate experience are not. For intellectual images and concepts need not correspond directly to experience. They often relate to it in a loose and general manner, as when a theory explains phenomena by means of much that is not observable.

Theoretical abstractions could not occur without this flexibility. But they are tentative, often followed by subsequent modifications. This exemplifies the changing cultural bias which supports even the most rigorous proofs. Thus Euclidean geometry gave way to other geometries in the nineteenth century. Likewise, Hipparchus and Ptolemy were once no less acceptable than Copernicus.

The Thinking Process

60. Determinate and Indeterminate

Any line derives its length from another line, which serves as its measure. Remove all reference to anything but the original line. And it will have no length. It will no longer be determinate. It becomes indeterminate. In other words, without reference to something else, the length of a line cannot be one inch or any other measure. Nor can the length of an isolated line segment be determined, unless it is referenced to the original line from which it is taken, to a fellow segment, or to something else which expresses an extension which might be considered a measure of length.

On the other hand, for something to be infinite, or not finite, it must bear no reference internally, externally, or even by suggestion to anything which is finite. To say that a line is infinite is equivalent to saying no individual aspect of that line is determinate—neither its width, length, texture, color, nor anything. In other words, it is not a line in any sense. Neither can there be infinities within infinities. But there can be indeterminacies within indeterminacies. For indeterminacies are finite, though the full character of their finitude remains undetermined.

The reader will recognize here a reference to the work of Georg Cantor.[51] The author does not wish to enter into dispute with the findings of this august mathematician, insofar as his assertions are mathematical. But the concept of a ma-

---

[51] See discussions of Cantor in Bertrand Russell's "Mathematics and the Metaphysicians" and in Hans Hahn's "Infinity."

terial infinity is inappropriate to philosophical discourse for the reason that it has no experiential basis.

Thus a correspondence between transfinite sets must be resolved experientially into a situation which is characteristic of indeterminate sets alone. This is because indeterminacies, which are all that can be figured forth in imagination, albeit incompletely, are finite and possess finite members.

For example, a set of real numbers, the members of which, when considered to be transfinite, are understood to exceed in correspondence those of a set of rational numbers, can, when the sets are considered to be indeterminate, only be more numerous by a finite, though indeterminate, extension, regardless of the indeterminate number of irrationals involved.

The reason for this is that individual numbers are finite. This includes irrational numbers. Though these are indeterminate in number, they are nonetheless individually finite.[52] Thus an accumulation of such finite extensions, both rational and irrational, results in finite extensions. So, if there are more numbers in the set of real numbers than in the set of rational numbers (though the precise number of either cannot be ascertained), the difference between the two sets constitutes a finite, albeit indeterminate, extension.

Nothing can be finite in one property but not in another—say in length but not breadth. Euclid's definition of a line

---

[52] As pointed out in previous chapters of this book and in the book, *The Limits of Reason,* by the present author, numbers are composed of arithmetical units. Though these units may have different magnitudes in different mathematical contexts, they are extensions. Also mentioned previously in this book and elsewhere is the fact that irrational numbers are approximations of rational numbers. They are approximations because they are indeterminate.

The Thinking Process

notwithstanding,[53] a finite length cannot be combined with no breadth, except by experientially unsupported supposition. For a line having no breadth, being nothing and having no extension, is not finite.

Such a line would not be present either to sensory experience or to a concrete imaginative representation. It must be supposed. And it must be represented graphically by what it is not: a line which exhibits breadth. Consequently, both a nothing and an infinity should be understood to be wholly unlike finitude.[54]

Something is wholly finite. Or it is wholly infinite. If it is finite, it can be broken down into smaller finite components or compounded with other finite entities into something greater. Or it may be equal to another. These are quantitative considerations. In addition, a finite entity must exhibit qualities. This is true even of those which are purely imaginative representations. For they must be composed of at least some mental impressions in order to be represented in the mind by an image.

Whereas, if the character of the infinite is brought into consideration, it is neither quantitatively divisible nor compoundable. Nor is it represented in qualitative terms. In fact, consciousness is the only example of infinity known to hu-

---

[53] *Euclid's Elements,* Book I, Definition 2: "A *line* is a breadthless length."

[54] Given the association of nothing with infinity, it might be inferred that consciousness, which is infinite, is nothing. But this is not the case. Nothing and consciousness are not discernible in sensory terms—i.e., by means of mental impressions and their associations. But consciousness is not nothing. For it is experienced. As for nothing, nothing is something finite which is deemed to be absent.

man awareness. The infinite bears a reference only to itself. Whereas a finite entity bears a reference to others of its kind.

61. Incompleteness

A system of thought like Euclid's *Elements* begins with axioms. The five common notions and five postulates of Book I provide the fundamental axioms of the system. It is also the case that the five common notions alone may be referred to as the axioms. And the postulates are designed to determine the extent and limits of practice. In either case, these ten principles act as rules of procedure. They are the formation rules of the system.

The postulates are set forth without variance. Or at least that was their original intention. But, since many people believe the 5th postulate looks more like a theorem than an axiom, this fundamental invariance has been questioned. The common notions, on the other hand, remain without variance, as they are derived from the manner in which the human mind works according to unities and pluralities. The intuitions of unity and plurality function in terms of units and multiples, which is what is expressed by the common notions.

But the definitions are different. They were originally presented in running narratives in the manner of prefaces,[55] and are provided in nine of the thirteen books of the *Ele-*

---

[55] *Euclid's Elements*, editor's footnote 1.

The Thinking Process

ments. For it is these which serve as the building blocks of the system, as opposed to the rules of procedure (or formation rules).

From these definitions, in accordance with the formation rules of the ten common notions and postulates, theorems may be derived. But what is important to note is that, unlike the common notions and the first four of the postulates, the definitions can be further reduced. For such is their nature that potentially they have no beginning or end.

This is because any definition can become an object of further investigation. In carrying out the investigation, the discovery will be made that it is possible to break the definition down into simpler definitions. In other words, these simpler definitions may be combined through formation rules, perhaps of a different character from those of the system, to produce the original definition. This process can be followed out to an indeterminate extent.

An example in support of these assertions can be drawn from the perfect circle. This is presented by Euclid as a definition.[56] And the possibility of its development is established by means of the axioms. The diameter is also defined.[57] It is defined in terms already set forth by the circle.

Now, since definitions have been placed in doubt as to their finality, this would make any one of them a potential theorem. For it can be composed of simpler definitions. Thus the diameter is defined in terms of the circle. And it is to be assumed that the circle must also have been derived from

---

[56] *Euclid's Elements*, Book I, Definition 15.
[57] *Euclid's Elements*, Book I, Definition 17.

other definitions, such as those of the radius and circumference.

A theorem is logically composite because it is derived from a combination of elements working together to form it. So, since a concept is also derived from a combination of elements, which are properties working together to form the concept, it can be assumed that a theorem is a concept.

This is permitted because any theorem or set of related theorems can be summed up as a concept, as in the conservation laws[58] of physical science being collectively a concept. So the derivation of a concept from its properties is equivalent to the derivation of a theorem from prior axioms and definitions. Even if a theorem is based upon prior theorems, these will eventually hark back to simple axioms and definitions.

A delineation of properties is the role of a concept's definition. In the concept which has been referred to as the "conservation laws," the properties are its specific applications, as in the laws of the conservation of mass and energy, electrical charge, linear momentum, etc., which substantiate the general principle. These define it. And their ultimate foundation is axiomatic and definitional. This equivalence between a concept and a theorem holds even if it concerns something as simple as a point or a line. The point and line, though stated as definitions by Euclid,[59] are theorems.

Thinking conceptually is a logical process, as opposed to a string of imaginative images, which forms a reverie. Conceptual thinking involves an intellectual judgment, however

---

[58] *Columbia Encyclopedia.*
[59] *Euclid's Elements*, Book I, Definitions 1 & 2.

The Thinking Process

subtle and spontaneous in character. In this way, one concept will transition to other concepts by means of an association or dissociation of definitions. So nothing can be thought about logically, including any theorem or its components, without the thoughts being concepts.

Let Euclid's definition of a circle be considered. It can be seen that he speaks of a circle in terms of its radius.

> A *circle* is a plane figure contained by one line such that all the straight lines falling upon it from one point among those lying within the figure are equal to one another.[60]

In addition, as can be deduced from his seventeenth definition, a diameter is equivalent to two radii.

> A *diameter* of the circle is any straight line drawn through the center and terminated in both directions by the circumference of the circle, and such a straight line also bisects the circle.[61]

So a question arises: are these definitions fundamental? For it can be seen that the seventeenth is founded upon a combination of the fifteenth and another definition, the sixteenth.

> And the point is called the *center* of the circle.[62]

---

[60] *Euclid's Elements*, Book I, Definition 15.
[61] *Euclid's Elements*, Book I, Definition 17.
[62] *Euclid's Elements*, Book I, Definition 16.

If the definition of a diameter is founded upon the definitions of a circle and the center of a circle, then clearly it is not fundamental in character. And the definition of the circle's center is also dependent upon the definition of the circle. So can the definition of the circle be founded upon other definitions as well?

Yes it can. For example, what is a straight line? To understand a straight line, one must have recourse to Euclid's first four definitions. And the first of these defines a point as "that which has no part."[63] But, to obtain a deeper understanding of Euclid's definition of a point, one must part company with Euclid's definitions in Book I of the *Elements*.

So, searching for the origin of the first definition, it must be asked: what does it mean for something to have no part? This requires getting a sense of what it means for something to have a part. Furthermore, what is a something? As can be seen, these questions lie beyond the definitional limits of Euclid's system.

The definitions of the *Elements*, along with the five postulates and five common notions, are the foundation for Euclid's system of geometry. They are fundamental. For they are not understood to have a prior origin beyond themselves. Yet, as has been shown, the definitions do. So why are they treated as fundamental?

The answer demonstrates the role of focus in thinking. Human beings cannot think without some kind of limitation to the range of their thought. That is, they cannot think without focus. So, to avoid an attempt to extend himself beyond any possible range of mental focus, a person simply decides

---

[63] *Euclid's Elements*, Book I, Definition 1.

The Thinking Process

not to pursue matters beyond a certain point, so that he can concentrate on the matter at hand. That is, he sets the range of his focus in such a way that it begins with what are treated as irreducible truths: the initial axioms and definitions.

But there are no irreducible definitions. Rather, the mind deliberately limits its thinking to systems built up with relatively small collections of axioms. And these are supplemented by what are treated as fundamental definitions, which function as building blocks for the system. If the mind did not limit itself in this way, then its system building would be endless. For it must reduce every definition to simpler elements.

So, if definitions are always reducible because other definitions must be found to support them, then new and different definitions must be hidden within every conceivable definition. However, this regression does have a limit. It is the finite character of the sum total of knowledge at any point in time. For this is limited.

Were it possible to embrace this total in a single thought system, it would be found to be integrated, or at least suggestive of a full integration. This would result from each set of definitions being defined by previous ones until, potentially, the earliest set of definitions is defined by the last, resulting in a circular chain of reason.

That this situation is avoided is due to the mind's limited range of focus, which prevents the creation of a circular system. It is also due to the fact that experience is ever-changing, deepening and extending the expression of knowledge, thus continually offering the potential for its further development.

So this much can be allowed: the mind may continue in its pursuit of an understanding of experience. But it may do this only insofar as it does not assume a total conquest of experience to be its goal. For were this possible, to reach absolute comprehension would demand a universally complete system of thought, which is infeasible both on the level of experience and of knowledge—the one unlimited, the other necessarily limited to avoid circularity.

Individual thought systems, such as physical science and biology, are separate because each of them lays its own characteristic (though illusory) claim to completeness. The different systems do not integrate with one another in a manner which would correlate to the totality of experience. In other words, they are not entirely reductionist in character because they are, in effect, independent maps of experience.

Thus it becomes increasingly clear that logical systems of thought arise from a limited focus operating in opposition to the potential circularity of reason. It is this limitation which allows for the mind's practical effectiveness. It exhibits a restricted range, which is in response to the infeasibility of a full compass of knowledge. The restricted range is combined with the unattainability of a complete embrace of experience. Between these tendencies lies the mind's capacity to think systematically.

These shortcomings work effectively together by allowing for the practical development of thought. For the mind's focus demands unity and integration. Hence the phenomenon of logical development. On the other hand, there is the broadly circular tendency of the intellect, which is inhibited by the limits of focus. And there is the continual growth of experience. Together, these opposing factors cause the mind

The Thinking Process

to yearn for a systematic completion of its thought which, though enticing, is unattainable.

In other words, if thinking were not uniform in the integration of its concepts, if the mind did not pursue a more comprehensive unity through that integration, if its concepts did not arise from simple origins subsequently compounded by reasoning into layers of complexity, and if those layers of complexity were not integrated with one another as well, it could not produce the intricate logical systems it produces.

But neither could a person believe in these systems, if his mind's focus encompassed every logical extension beyond the train of reason under immediate consideration. For then he would see the circular track of his own reason. So this must be said: due to its integration of concepts being confined within the limits of mental focus, all logical relations cannot be entertained at once.

In addition, due to the ever-unfolding complexity of experience, neither can they be known. Both these limiting factors are necessary to the successful functioning of the mind, the first to give its systems a comprehensible structure, the second to nourish an expectation of further development.

62. Imagination

Imagination involves both analysis and synthesis. That is, to analyze it selects properties. And to synthesize it combines them within open thoughts. Open thoughts may be similar to concepts inasmuch as they can be groupings of properties. But they are not closed by definitions. They are therefore not concepts, but sets of images.

A definition both emphasizes certain properties and insures that they are not subject to change, thus rendering a concept accessible to logical operations. But open thoughts are independent imagery, which, being undefined, remain subject to change. Thus they cannot enter into logical operations.

Imaginative thinking can involve a selection, combination, separation again, and recombination of properties within imagery. This process, so long as it is maintained, can lead to unending modifications, as the mind transitions from prior images to new. But a concept must be rendered into open thoughts (i.e., undefined imagery) for purposes of imaginative play. In other words, its definition must be set aside so its image content will be set free. For imagination must have no limits. It cannot be bound by the rules of logic. However, the price of this freedom is a lack of precision.

It becomes clear from this that any closed thought may be brought under the play of imagination simply by rendering it an open thought. As a closed thought, or concept, it is a prior creation of imagination which has been raised to the level of reason. As an open thought, it is being returned to imaginative play as a set of images.

This process functions much in the manner of a poet's use of simile, metaphor, or unexpected juxtapositions of images. A poet's effective use of these is achieved through a free association which is brought about between one word's connotations and those of another word or group of words. Free association releases powers of suggestion. The suggestions are images, often visualizations, which, if

The Thinking Process

conceptualized, are brought under definitions, which again are expressed in words.

But they are not conceptualized because suggestion is the essence of poetry. This is why the full meaning of a good poem will not be stated or directly represented anywhere within that work. In fact, it may not be possible to state or represent the poem's meaning by any means other than that which the poem exhibits.

Beyond the free play of imagination, there is a more restrictive, hybrid process involving imagination. It is induction, which employs both imagination and deductive reason. The constituent elements of an induction are images representing physical experience. Multiple images functioning as properties are subsequently formed into a concept. And, if faithfully representative of the experience, as they should be in an inductive process, they are organized in accordance with that experience.

Now in imaginative free play images may be drawn from memory. For memory is the principal source of material for imaginative free play—in fact, for all thought, imaginative or conceptual. So memory is also a storehouse of concepts. Thus a reference to experience can often be ignored.

But, given that induction arises from the imagery of physical experience and attempts to remain faithful to it, it must be regarded as a process that involves an association of properties which takes place in a more restricted sense than in imaginative free play. It is not a free play of imagination, but a recognition of the order in which properties appear in physical experience. So it is in no way random.

First, there is an encounter with individual mental impressions in physical experience. And it is imagination which recognizes order among these impressions. Such order is the imagery of perception. Secondly, it is noted that these images are also encountered in associations. So they are recog-recognized as properties. These are formed into closed thoughts in order to function as logically accessible concepts.

The third step is deductive reason performing logical functions. But this reasoning will occur without certainty. In other words, it will be probabilistic in character. This results from the fact that, though the order of material experience may be consistent, it is never demonstrably necessary.

A closed thought employed in deductive reason does not yield to a modification of properties within itself. For the terms of a proposition are not altered in their properties by reasoning. Modification of properties only occurs in imagination, where, by means of association, mental impressions move freely between images, thus altering properties.

Reason, as a late stage of induction, differs from the earlier imaginative steps of the process. The preliminary imaginative stages involve a recognition of the order of mental impressions within properties, and of an association of properties within an object. And it is these which are followed by concept formation, where properties are set by definition. Concept formation facilitates reasoning, which does not alter the properties within the concepts, except where imagination takes over to form a new concept.

But deductive reason need not serve solely as a means for completing an inductive process. Thus it is not restricted to probabilistic thinking. It can stand alone, as is the case when mathematical operations, the theoretical integration of scientific observations, and speculative philosophy proceed strictly according to deduction.

The Thinking Process

However, reason does borrow its capacity for making logical transitions from the imaginative faculty of analysis and synthesis. For the transitions are characterized by forms of association and dissociation, as in the use of "all," "some," "no," and "not all." Imagination is the faculty which governs both. But within reason it works with concepts, or closed thoughts.

A statement thus becomes a classification within which its subject and predicate terms are held as subordinate classifications. And a logical sequence of statements recombines the terms within one statement with those of another. The statements function as classifications, just as their terms do. But they can be broken down into their terms.

Whereas the terms cannot be broken down. And, since these associative operations employ the terms intact, rather than separating properties from them, none of the terms are internally altered, though the statements are. Each of the terms is held in a completed state throughout the variation in statements.

So, since any analysis and synthesis such as the above must occur by means of dissociation and association, it can be seen that the reasoning process itself does employ imagination in its logical transitions. But it is carried out in a more guarded way, dissociating or associating the properties of terms in relation to those of other terms without altering them within the original terms.

Thus it is imagination which brings concepts into association with one another in new ways by observing or positing relations between their properties. But the process is different from that of free imagery. Under the control of reason, imagination does not attempt to alter a concept in any way, except when creating and inserting entirely new concepts into the reasoning process. Rather, it makes associations between the properties within different existing concepts, while keeping the properties of each concept intact.

But it may make associations or dissociations partly or wholly. The combinations and separations of meaning are made between complete concepts, rather than between their properties alone. Yet it is the latter which are the actual means of this association or dissociation. So, when one concept is partially or wholly predicated or denied of another, its total meaning is either partially or wholly associated with or dissociated from the other.

Quantifiers, be they universal or existential, do no more than indicate relations of quantity (part and whole), and specify to what quantity of the subject the predication is to apply or not apply. It is a matter of associations or disassociations of whole concepts within statements and between statements. The process is deductive when it proceeds strictly according to these rules of logic.

63. Human Awareness

Descartes states in *Rules for the Direction of the Mind* that the terms "body" and "extension" cannot be visually separated by imagination. In his view, to imagine an extension alone is to imagine an extended body. It cannot be

The Thinking Process

otherwise.[64] In post-Kantian philosophy, it can be asserted that this is due to the phenomenal representation of material experience. Human knowledge is limited to the phenomenal. So is imagination.

Imagination cannot represent an extension independent of body. Nor can it represent a body independent of extension. This is because the imagination is not prior to the phenomenal representation. Rather, it is involved in it. Thus it is also dependent upon it. Or, to be precise, it is dependent upon the receipt of its constituent elements, the mental impressions. For it can only construct images which are drawn from the material which consciousness presents to awareness.

Nevertheless, though the mind cannot visualize a body independently from an extension, it can use its associative powers to compare the images it creates. These images are the phenomenal representations. In forming them, the mind recognizes that extensions have something in common: body. For extensions exclude one another in mental and physical space. And exclusion of other bodies is what characterizes a body. So body is identified as a property of each extension. Moreover, it is a general property. For it is interchangeable with the concept "extension."

The mind is further enabled to form a concept of extension by means of the constituent properties supporting its representation of body. These constituent properties are the elements of the general property "body." Interestingly, one of these is shape, or figure. And another is extension. Hence extension becomes a property of itself as a constituent property of its general property "body."

---

[64] René Descartes, *Rules for the Direction of the Mind*, Rule XIV.

So these constituent properties are properties of the extension. And they are the properties of body. Thus they become the basis of a definition of both extension and body, each exhibiting the other as a property. In this way, "body" can be intellectually abstracted from "extension." And that is what creates the illusion of the separation of body from extension.

A definition is supported by images. For it must be, however much the imagery may lie in the shadowy background of its verbal expression. So, if the mind wishes to conceptually represent either a body or an extension, it will conceive it as supported by properties. Thus the same properties will support the definitions of both, with the exception that "body" supports extension and "extension" supports body.

But, while the images representing these properties are products of imagination, they are constructed from mental impressions which are received without the agency of imagination. For the mental impressions are prior to the operations of imagination. Only subsequent to receiving them does the imagination form images from them.

So mental impressions are made present to awareness without the agency of imagination. And, because the imagination forms images by means of the three intuitions (unity, plurality, and totality), which function subsequent to the presentation of the mental impressions, the origin of the impressions is hidden behind a veil. For the veil is an imaginative construct which immediately intervenes to produce experience.

However, reason, the instrument of intellectual awareness, is able to make adjustments to this original imaginative representation. It may interpret it. But reason only reaches its full capacity with the maturing of the mind. This is why the

The Thinking Process

world does not look the same to a child as to an adult, or even to two adults who have not undergone the same intellectual development or been educated in the same way.

Bibliography

Aquinas, Thomas. "On Being and Essence." In *Selected Writings of Saint Thomas Aquinas,* translated by Robert P. Goodwin. New York: The Bobbs-Merrill Company, Inc., 1965.

Archimedes. "Measurement of a Circle." In *Euclid, Archimedes, Apollonius of Perga, Nicomachus, Vol. 11, Great Books of the Western World*, translated by Sir Thomas L. Heath. Chicago: Encyclopedia Britannica, Inc., 1952.

Aristotle. "Logic." In *Aristotle I, Vol. 8, Great Books of the Western World*, translated by E. M. Edghill, A. J. Jenkinson, G. R. G. Mure, and W. A. Pickard-Cambridge. Chicago: Encyclopedia Britannica, Inc., 1952.

———. "Metaphysics." In *Aristotle I, Vol. 8, Great Books of the Western World*, translated by W. D. Ross. Chicago: Encyclopedia Britannica, Inc., 1952.

———. "On the Soul." In *Aristotle I, Vol 8, Great Books of the Western World*, translated by J. A. Smith. Chicago: Encyclopedia Britannica, Inc., 1952.

———. "Physics." In *Aristotle I, Vol 8, Great Books of the Western World*, translated by R. P. Hardie and R. K. Gaye. Chicago: Encyclopedia Britannica, Inc., 1952.

Berkeley, George. "The Principles of Human Knowledge." In *Locke, Berkeley, Hume, Vol. 35, Great Books of the Western World*. Chicago: Encyclopedia Britannica, Inc., 1952.

———. " Three Dialogues between Hylas and Philonous." In *Locke, Berkeley, Hume, Vol. 35, Great Books of the*

Western World. Chicago: Encyclopedia Britannica, Inc., 1952.

Columbia Encyclopedia, edited by Paul Lagassé. New York: Columbia University Press, 2000.

Dedekind, Richard. "Continuity and Irrational Numbers." In *Essays on the Theory of Numbers,* translated by Wooster Woodruff Beman. New York: Dover Publications, Inc., 1963.

Descartes, René. "Rules for the Direction of the Mind." In *Descartes, Spinoza, Vol. 31, Great Books of the Western World*, translated by Elizabeth S. Haldane and G. R. T. Ross. Chicago: Encyclopedia Britannica, Inc., 1952.

Einstein, Albert and Leopold Infeld. *The Evolution of Physics.* New York: Simon & Schuster, 1938.

———. *Relativity, The Special and the General Theory*, translated by Robert W. Lawson. New York: Penguin, 2006.

Euclid. *Euclid's Elements,* translated by Thomas L. Heath. Santa Fe: Green Lion Press, 2010.

Hahn, Hans. "Infinity." In *The World of Mathematics, Vol. 3,* edited by James R. Newman. New York: Simon and Schuster, 1956.

Harvey, William. "An Anatomical Disquisition on the Motion of the Heart and Blood in Animals." In *Gilbert, Galileo, Harvey, Vol. 28, Great Books of the Western World,* translated by Robert Willis. Chicago: Encyclopedia Britannica, Inc., 1952.

Heath, Thomas L. *A Manual of Greek Mathematics.* Mineola: Dover Publications, Inc., 2003.

Hume, David. "An Enquiry Concerning Human Understanding." In *Locke, Berkeley, Hume, Vol. 35, Great*

Books of the Western World. Chicago: Encyclopedia Britannica, Inc., 1952.

———. *A Treatise of Human Nature,* edited by L. A. Selby-Bigge. New York: Oxford University Press, 1973.

James, William. "Does 'Consciousness' Exist?" In *William James: Writings 1902-1910.* New York: The Library of America, 1987.

Kant, Immanuel. "The Critique of Pure Reason." In *Kant, Vol. 42, Great Books of the Western World*, translated by J. M. D. Meiklejohn. Chicago: Encyclopedia Britannica, Inc., 1952.

Kuhn, Thomas S. *The Structure of Scientific Revolutions.* Chicago: University of Chicago Press, 1996.

Locke, John. "An Essay Concerning Human Understanding." In *Locke, Berkeley, Hume, Vol. 35, Great Books of the Western World.* Chicago: Encyclopedia Britannica, Inc., 1952.

Mill, John Stuart. "On Liberty." In *American State Papers, The Federalist, J. S. Mill, Vol. 43, Great Books of the Western World.* Chicago: Encyclopedia Britannica, Inc., 1953.

———. *System of Logic: Ratiocinative and Inductive.* Toronto: University of Toronto Press, 1974.

Newton, Isaac. "Mathematical Principles of Natural Philosophy." In *Newton, Huygens, Vol. 34, Great Books of the Western World.* Chicago: Encyclopedia Britannica, Inc., 1952.

Pavlov, Ivan Petrovich. "Scientific Study of the So-called Psychical Processes in the Higher Animals." In *Natural Science, Vol. 8, Gateway to the Great Books,* translated

The Thinking Process

    by W. Horsley Gantt. Chicago: Encyclopedia Britannica, Inc., 1952.

Plato. "The Dialogues of Plato." In *Plato, Vol. 7, Great Books of the Western World*, translated by Benjamin Jowett. Chicago: Encyclopedia Britannica, Inc., 1952.

Pope, Alexander. "Engraved on the Collar of a Dog, Which I Gave to His Royal Highness." In *Immortal Poems of the English Language,* edited by Oscar Williams. New York: Simon & Schuster, 1952.

Russell, Bertrand. "Mathematics and the Metaphysicians." In *The World of Mathematics, Vol. 3,* edited by James R. Newman. New York: Simon and Schuster, 1956.

Schopenhauer, Arthur. *The World as Will and Representation, Vols. 1 & 2*, translated by E. F. J. Payne. New York: Dover Publications, Inc., 1966.

Tollefson, George Lowell. *The Immaterial Structure of Human Experience*. Santa Fe: Palo Flechado Press, 2019.

———. *The Limits of Reason*. Santa Fe: Palo Flechado Press, 2020.

George Lowell Tollefson

Index of Names

Aquinas, 143, 143 (n. 31)
Archimedes, 129
Aristarchus of Samos, 129
Aristotle, 4, 4 (n. 1), 68, 160–61, 160 (n. 32), 177, 177 (n. 36), 214 (n. 44)
Berkeley, 183, 183 (n. 40)
Cantor, 246, 246 (n. 51)
Copernicus, 133, 245
Dedekind, 94 (n. 22)
Descartes, 261, 262 (n. 64)
Einstein, 130
Euclid, 93 (n. 18), 94, 94 (n. 19–21), 130, 140, 155, 171, 180, 245, 247, 248 (n.53), 249, 249 (n. 55), 250–251, 250 (n. 56–57), 251 (n. 59), 252, 252 (n. 60–62), 253, 253 (n. 63)
Euler, 23, 171
Galileo, 129
Harvey, 165–167, 165 (n. 33)
Heath, 129 (n. 29)
Hipparchus, 129, 245
Hume, 54, 55 (n. 11), 63, 63 (n. 12), 88, 88 (n. 15), 183, 183 (n. 39), 235, 235 (n. 48–49)
James, 10 (n. 2), 18, 18 (n. 5)
Kant, 55, 183, 183 (n. 41), 262
Kepler, 129
Kuhn, 237 (n. 50)
Locke, 182, 182 (n. 38)
Mendeleev, 171

The Thinking Process

Mill, 8
Newton, 62, 71, 129
Pavlov, 88, 88 (n. 16)
Plato, 14, 14 (n. 4), 167, 167 (n. 34), 168, 175–177, 179
Pope, 131, 132 (n. 30)
Ptolemy, 129, 245
Schopenhauer, 12, 12 (n. 3)
Tollefson, 183 (n. 42)

www.ingramcontent.com/pod-product-compliance
Lightning Source LLC
Chambersburg PA
CBHW071958110526
44592CB00012B/1129